I0465164

LEADERSHIP
NONNEGOTIABLES

*Personal Character, Leadership
Talent, and Management Skill*

T. S. MARSHALL, PHD
with
Richard W. Stackman, PhD

authorHOUSE®

AuthorHouse™
1663 Liberty Drive
Bloomington, IN 47403
www.authorhouse.com
Phone: 1 (800) 839-8640

© 2017 T. S. Marshall & Associates, Inc. All rights reserved.

No part of this book may be reproduced, stored in a retrieval system, or transmitted by any means without the written permission of the author.

Published by AuthorHouse 03/23/2017

ISBN: 978-1-5246-7545-5 (sc)
ISBN: 978-1-5246-7544-8 (e)

Library of Congress Control Number: 2017903741

Print information available on the last page.

This book is printed on acid-free paper.

Because of the dynamic nature of the Internet, any web addresses or links contained in this book may have changed since publication and may no longer be valid. The views expressed in this work are solely those of the author and do not necessarily reflect the views of the publisher, and the publisher hereby disclaims any responsibility for them.

CONTENTS

FOREWORD

There is no magic formula, manual, or predetermined path to becoming a leader. To succeed at leading, one should approach the endeavor as a unique journey, not a set destination. Leading others is personal (and social). One's success depends on knowing oneself, being self-aware and self-motivated, and engaging the talents of others to achieve leadership outcomes. Leadership is a collaborative effort. When a situation calls for you to step up—to lead—you must be ready, willing, and able to lead. So, are you? If not, or unsure, then the lessons in this book will prepare you for that moment when you do step up to lead. If yes, there are always precious lessons to learn regarding the whole of leadership that will enhance your effectiveness to lead.

Simply put, this book provides aspiring or experienced leaders with a well-thought-out discussion of personal character, leadership talent, and management skill in a distinctive way. It presents practiced perspectives, skilled insights, and proficient narratives intended to resonate with every reader. The chosen title is not arbitrary, especially the word *nonnegotiables*. While personal character, leadership talent, and management skill—we believe—are necessary for leadership success, each is not sufficient on its own to secure such success.

Admittedly, when it comes to learning about leadership, there is much to choose from; the topic is a library unto itself. Leadership is one of the most studied—if not the most studied—concepts in the organization sciences, and it continues to be discussed and debated among practitioners and researchers alike from the business, nonprofit, health-care, or government sectors. Moreover, there is no monopoly on one's understanding of leadership. If one took the time to read as many books on leadership as possible, the likely conclusion is this: much of what is said is similar. A quote attributed to Mo Udall aptly applies: "Everything has been said but not everyone has said it."

Though "everything has been said" (figuratively speaking), we do believe *our saying it*—supported by the thinking of others in the field—advances the literature as it applies to character, leadership (and leading), and management (and managing). As a result, we further believe you will find the reading to be informative, instructive, and thought provoking.

This book, *Leadership Nonnegotiables*, is a companion book to Steve's earlier work titled *Competent Leadership.*[1] Leadership competence revolves around one's personal style, one's relationships, and how one communicates, motivates, resolves conflict, and makes decisions. What went unsaid in *Competent Leadership* is the foundation for this book. The focus of *Leadership Nonnegotiables* is what we consider the very core of leading—personal character, leadership talent, and management skill. One does not lead in isolation. Leadership occurs among and with others, and those others expect leaders to be of character and imbued with talent and skill.

Dr. Marshall (Steve) and I have known each other for more than twenty years, having met as faculty members at the University of Washington, Tacoma, in 1996. As our careers diverged, our friendship has deepened. While Steve toils primarily in the world of practice and I (Richard) in the world of academia, we consider ourselves both students and teachers. We continue to learn from and with each other. This book captures our discussions on leadership over the years. We have not compromised our beliefs as we endeavored to blend our knowledge and experience in order to speak with one coherent voice. We have marshaled (pun intended) our character, talent, and skill in writing and editing this book. We had a great time doing just that.

---

[1] T. S. Marshall, *Competent Leadership: Presenting the knowledge to lead, along with the practical lessons and experience to do it well* (Chicago: Green Ivy, 2015).

As you set off to read *Leadership Nonnegotiables*, it bears repeating what Steve wrote in *Competent Leadership*: "Just like there is no one-style-fits-all approach to leadership, reliance on only one book, one voice, one approach is ill advised. Want to become a better leader? Read whatever you can on leadership; learn what you can; and practice, practice, practice." To that passage we add that you also reflect, reflect, reflect on a daily basis with respect to how you continually develop your character, talent, and skill as a leader.

—Richard W. Stackman, PhD
San Francisco, California

Acknowledgments

First, to my dear friend and longtime colleague, Richard W. Stackman, PhD. Thank you for your contribution to this book. Your collaboration, insight, and prose were always welcomed and immensely valuable. You made this a better book!

I wish, too, to thank my wife, Sandra, for her encouragement and support in writing this book. Her patience and understanding were greatly appreciated.

Finally, many thanks to those who were the first to review my manuscript: Jo VanDerSnick, Howard Schussler, Cheryl Ann Graf, and Marc Correa. Their professional perspectives were immensely helpful.

CHAPTER 1

LEADERSHIP NONNEGOTIABLES

Therese is a regional director of a large multinational corporation. Over the years, she developed trusted relationships with peers, union members, stakeholders, and staff, and together they amassed solid records of achievement. Most everyone talked about how they enjoyed working with Therese. Regional management, teamwork, and resolve were evident, and people felt valued and seemed eager to come to work. Therese, too, was gratified that years of collaboration and hard work by her and others was paying off. All things considered, it could not be better.

Within months of Therese's third year as regional director, she was asked to relocate to a region troubled by dismal performance, a distrusting union relationship, and a disheartened staff. Given her track record, senior executives were hopeful that Therese could turn things around; namely, that she could improve performance, morale, and customer satisfaction in a region beset with performance problems. To Therese, the move was unexpected and, frankly, unasked for, but she felt there was little she could do. To decline could jeopardize future career opportunities; to accept could mean her demise. You see, the troubled region had a reputation of ending directors' careers—proof of this was made evident once again by the ouster of that region's current director, her (to be) predecessor. Also troublesome were her thoughts of how the move would affect her family; this was the cause of much apprehension. Ultimately, Therese accepted the opportunity and began preparing for the move.

Determined to get off to a good start, Therese reached out to the regional director being replaced to ask for his insights, understandings, and perspectives on the region's strengths and weaknesses, as well as the most urgent issues facing the region. In addition, she asked for a list of key stakeholders, staff, and union members that she could reach out to to get their perspectives. After several phone calls, Therese knew she had a lot of work to do; while the departing director cited staff resistance and union roadblocks for performance shortfalls, others cited director distrust and mismanagement for failed performance. It was a bitter blame game—one characterized by name-calling and finger-pointing.

When Therese arrived at her new region, the climate was one of reservation; some staff seemed standoffish toward her, while others were polite at best. Expectedly, talk about Therese had preceded her too. Just as she had called ahead to get information about the region and staff, those there had done likewise about her. The buzz they had received regarding her was good; people had spoken of her as being trustworthy, talented, and skilled, and were sad to see her leave.

Even so, building connections at the new region did not come easy. Each workday, Therese spent an hour or so getting to know the people and the work they did—trying to build relationships one conversation at a time. Therese's biggest hurdle, at least initially, was overcoming the shadow of distrust, broken promises, and damaged relationships that had built up over the years. It was evident to Therese that people came to work and did their jobs—for the most part—yet they were not engaged. Though she was not her predecessor, many people in the region viewed her in a similar light. Few saw her any differently from past directors. Therese soon realized she had to not only build trust and credibility in her, the *person*, but she had to restore trust and credibility in her office, the *regional director position*, as well. The two were inseparable. Furthermore, it seemed to Therese that there was a prevailing sense of distrust in most everything and everyone in the region. Much work in this area needed to be done.

In time, people slowly began to open up as Therese listened to and acted upon their concerns and recommendations for improvements. Relationships formed, mutual confidences grew, and people began focusing on their work instead of the distractions of the past. Therese and others could feel a shift in momentum. After a year in the making, not all due to Therese's actions alone, regional performance, morale, and customer satisfaction began steadily improving. And with these improvements, so too did Therese's personal and position credibility grow, as did region trust and teamwork. Though still fragile—as past slights, injustices, and other memories take time to fade—dialogue, mutual respect, and, most importantly, teamwork became the norm. Moreover, region performance was no longer lingering at the corporate bottom, union-management relationships were on the rise, trust and credibility regionwide were becoming noticeable, and staff no longer talked about what was. The region was focused on moving forward—results.

In this chapter, we will examine leading and managing, introduce the leadership nonnegotiables, and test some leadership and management premises presented by the author.

LEADING VERSUS MANAGING

To understand leadership (and leading) one must appreciate its relationship to management (and managing). Therese's story evokes images of both leading and managing. Management and leadership are not synonymous, and, though tempting, the two words should not be used interchangeably. Instead, leading and managing are distinct yet complementary.[2] Think of the two this way: where managers promote stability, leaders press for change; where managers ensure organizations continue to operate; leaders keep organizations evolving. Therefore, while managing is about planning and budgeting, organizing and staffing, and controlling and problem solving; leading is about setting a vision, aligning people, creating coalitions, and motivating and inspiring. Thus, leadership is about preparing organizations for change and then helping those organizations achieve desired outcomes. Only those organizations that embrace and integrate managing and leading thrive. Table 1.1 provides a summary of the leader-manager distinction.

---

[2] J. P. Kotter, "What leaders really do," *Harvard Business Review*, December 2011.

Table 1.1: Leading vs. Managing

	LEADERS	MANAGERS
Seek situations that create:	Change	Stability
Focus goals on:	Improvement	Continuity
Base power on:	Personal influence	Hierarchical authority
Seek outcome buy-in from:	Commitment	Compliance
Drive performance through:	Support, development	Rewards, discipline
Define success through:	Employee commitment, mutuality and trust, effectiveness	Maintaining quality, stability, consistency, efficiency

Therese, it could be argued, demonstrated strong management and leadership given the opportunity presented to her. Her actions were reflective of good management as she established a degree of order and consistency for those employed in the region, *and* she demonstrated strong leadership by bringing about change to the unit, thus improving the region's performance and positive viability. However, it cannot be assumed a given individual can be simultaneously a leader and manager in all situations across time. We are all aware of individuals who are/were viewed as successful leaders in one situation but not another. *It is naïve to believe that all-encompassing leadership and all-encompassing management prowess are found in one individual.* Though trite, it takes a village of individuals—leaders and managers, as well as leaders who can manage, and managers who can lead—to build, sustain, and change an organization. Everyone is given the opportunity to lead, and everybody is expected to lead. What is important to remember is that success in today's workplace is dependent on partnerships among individuals who work together. Leadership, and the responsibilities of leadership, is shared.

Therese's story illustrates three nonnegotiables that are crucial to leadership: *personal character, leadership talent,* and *management skill* (see figure 1.1). These nonnegotiables represent the beliefs that: (1) we expect our leaders to be good people, (2) we expect them to lead people effectively, and (3) we expect them to manage things efficiently. In other words, leaders must be seen as **credible, capable,** and **competent.** These nonnegotiables are not independent components of leadership; rather, they are interdependent. It is the presence of all three nonnegotiables that unite to inspire and achieve *leadership outcomes*—influencing others to pursue a shared goal. Any nonnegotiable that is found lacking will diminish one's ability to lead and, subsequently, reduce the likelihood of achieving a successful leadership outcome.

Figure 1.1: Leadership Nonnegotiables

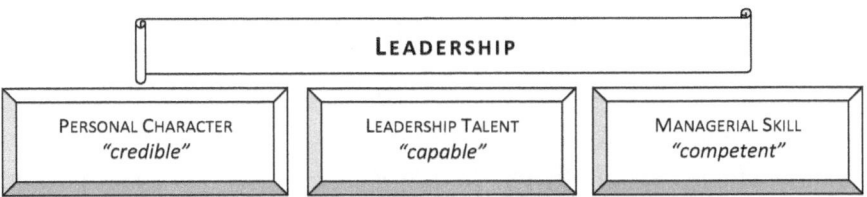

The leadership nonnegotiables are interdependent, concurrent, and mutually supporting.

Before discussing the nonnegotiables in more detail, it is important to note another key difference between leading and management. The best managers ensure day-to-day operations are executed effectively and efficiently by managing (or controlling) the inevitable ups and downs of work flow and performance. *Managers*, with whom accountability is vested, reside within an organization's hierarchy.[3] By virtue of their position—be it as a line supervisor, a regional manager, or a vice president—they have positional power. In other words, they can make individuals comply through use of legitimate power as well as through use of rewards, discipline, etc.

---

[3] E. Jaques, "In praise of hierarchy," *Harvard Business Review,* 1990.

Leaders, however, extend beyond the organizational hierarchy. Leaders rely on personal power or influence.[4] Instead of merely complying with the exercise of management (and the management structure), people commit to a leader and his or her vision. Ideally, the exercise of compliance as a means of achieving leadership outcomes should be the exception, not the practice. In Therese's case, she inherited a region of individuals who were complying, dare we say barely complying. Yet, over time, Therese was able draw the region's stakeholders, union members, and staff together to build a shared vision toward accomplishing more collectively as a team than anyone could accomplish alone. Dee Ward Hock, founder and former CEO of the Visa credit card association, had this to say about leadership: "Control is not leadership; management is not leadership; leadership is leadership." Though self-defining, it makes the point.

While there is no substitute for *personal character* (as it must always be present), elements of *leadership talent* and *management skill* can be shared or distributed among individuals. This practice should not be surprising, as it is common for staff collectively to have more expertise and greater capability than their leader alone. Though all three nonnegotiables must be present to lead, it is not necessary that the leader do them all. It is, however, essential that a leader recognizes the existence of a need and ensures that a given nonnegotiable is fulfilled (by them or by someone else). To that end, the presence of the three leadership nonnegotiables—blended or sequenced—encourages achievement of leadership outcomes and lessens overreliance on compulsory ways. As a result, leaders and followers must recognize and accept that the majority of *leadership outcomes* require teamwork—everyone contributing toward a shared goal or purpose. One final, and necessary, note on this topic: while leaders are not expected to know all and do all, they are expected to do their share of the work.

---

[4] Other works relative to this discussion: *The Bases of Social Power,* J. R. P. French and B. Raven (New York: Harper & Row, 1959); and *Management of Organizational Behavior:* Leading Human Resources, P. Hersey and K. H. Blanchard (Englewood Cliffs, NJ: Prentice-Hall, 1982).

TEST OF ASSERTIONS

Given the assertion that all three nonnegotiables are required to lead and, thus, vital to achieving leadership outcomes, let us examine each one more closely and test that assertion:

> ➤ Personal character (**You**): Personal character is the "you" you project for all to see; it comprises the mental and emotional qualities, characteristics, and attributes that make you distinct and is influenced by your life's experiences, culture, beliefs, education, gender, ethnicity, and so on. Norman Schwartzkopf, a US Army general, wrote this about character: "Leadership is a potent combination of strategy and character. But if you must be without one, be without strategy." The focus of personal character is "you"—*leaders should be good people too.*[5]

"**YOU**"

> For example, a person may have exceptional *talent* and *skill*, but if he or she will lie to you and throw you under the bus if it will advance his or her position, then few (if any one) will willingly follow them.

> *Leadership Talent* ☑   *Managerial Skill* ☑   *Personal Character* ☒

> Poor *personal character* limits influence; leadership outcomes suffer. *Personal character* cannot be outsourced; it is a personal responsibility.

---

[5] T. A. Wright and J. C. Quick in their article titled "The role of character in ethical leadership research," *The Leadership Quarterly*, 2011, 976, write: "A character-based leader is best viewed as an agent for moral change. To that end, a character-based leader is one with the requisite self-control (moral discipline) to selflessly act on their own volition (moral autonomy) to inspire, sustain and transform the attitudes and beliefs of both themselves and their followers. Best viewed as providing an overarching moral compass, the character-based leader has the perspective to continuously strive to move their team or organization beyond narrow, self-interest pursuits toward the attainment of common good goals (moral attachment)."

➢ Leadership talent (**People**): Grace Murray Hopper, an American computer scientist and US Navy rear admiral, said, "You manage things; you lead people." So true. Leadership talent comprises the *knowledge, skills, ability,* and *willingness* to lead; it is not based upon where you sit (or what position you hold in the hierarchy) but upon what you do. Leaders must be good readers of people and able to customize leadership styles to meet specific individual and/or group needs. The focus of leadership talent is "people"— *you lead people.*

For example, *character* and *skill (at managing)* can be undeniable, but if one's *leadership talent* is regarded as weak or lacking, then no one will want to follow. Is he or she a good person and a skillful manager? Sure. A leader? No.

Personal Character ☑ *Managerial Skill* ☑ *Leadership Talent* ☒

Meager *leadership talent* sidetracks purpose; desired outcomes suffer. Until *leadership talent* is capable, get help from informal leaders to fill gaps.

➢ Managerial skill (**Things**): It is the understanding and management of the system of service, production, and delivery that supports performance. The focus of management skill is "things" (e.g., staffing, strategic planning, budgeting, managing with data)—*you manage things.*

"THINGS"
Staffing,
Planning,
Budgeting,
Measures

For example, a person has outstanding *personal character* and robust *leadership talent,* but his or her lack of *management skill* has resulted in vague taskings, costly delays, and mounting frustration. Mismanagement is driving talent out the door.

Personal Character ☑   *Leadership Talent* ☑   *Management Skill* ☒

Inadequate *management skills* hinder performance, which results in leadership outcomes suffering. Like above, get help from others who can help manage.

The very interdependencies of these leadership nonnegotiables make it difficult to isolate one without consideration of the others. Moreover, varying contexts and environments require blending or sequencing the three nonnegotiables to achieve optimal outcomes. Judgment is required.

Finally, all three nonnegotiables require balanced cognitive and emotional abilities. It is the presence of both *cognitive ability* (e.g., the general mental capability to think, reason, plan, solve programs, comprehend complex ideas, and learn from experience) and *emotional intelligence* (e.g., the ability to recognize and manage one's own emotions, recognize others' emotions, and handle the interaction of both)[6] that enables each of us to navigate opportunities and challenges. These abilities provide the framework for developing and exercising the leadership nonnegotiables. And like leadership and management, one is not a substitute for the other. Without the presence of both *cognitive ability* and *emotional intelligence*, one will be challenged to meaningfully recognize and appropriately respond to what is seen and heard. The presence of both allows us to recognize context, to understand as well as be understood, and to remain composed under pressure.

With the emergence of *emotional intelligence* in the 1990s, we have witnessed a proliferation of other "intelligences." Three such intelligences are worth noting. *Social (interpersonal) intelligence*, which dates back to the 1920s[7], is the capacity to effectively navigate and negotiate complex social relationships and environments. *Contextual intelligence* is the ability to understand the limits of our knowledge and to adapt that knowledge to an environment different from the one in which it was developed. Finally, *cultural intelligence* is the capability to relate and work effectively across cultures.

We must take into account that one's cognitive abilities and the above-mentioned intelligences can—and should—be developed over time.

---

[6] See seminal works related to emotional intelligence: "The intelligence of emotional intelligence," J. D. Mayer and P. Salovey, Intelligence, 1993; "Five components of emotional intelligence at work," D. Goleman, *Harvard Business Review,* 2004.
[7] E. L. Thorndike, "Intelligence and its uses," *Harper's Magazine,* 1920.

Moreover, cognitive ability, and emotional, social, contextual, and cultural intelligences are necessary for anyone to lead and/or manage successfully. However, given their definitions, the presence of contextual and cultural intelligence better distinguishes those who can lead from those who can merely manage.

In the next three chapters, the three leadership nonnegotiables are individually addressed. Before focusing on personal character, leadership talent, and managerial skill, let us take a moment to review some key points. The focus of this book is about leadership in its fullest context, and it is about how one can continue to develop as a leader so he or she can lead when called upon to do so (or when he or she realizes someone needs to step forward and lead, and then does so). Keep in mind that the multiple roles and tasks within organizations make it impractical for one individual to serve as an *all-encompassing* leader—to be all things to all people. Even Therese was but one individual in the transformation of her region. Organizations rely on individuals willing and able to lead when the opportunity presents itself.

To borrow a very popular quote: "Leadership is a journey, not a destination. It is a marathon, not a sprint. It is a process, not an outcome."[8] This journey is also deeply personal and, at the same time, socially rooted. We develop our capacity to lead through personal growth. It involves being honest about our limitations and then addressing those limitations while learning to partner with others—*leadership strength comes from building relationships, partnerships, and coalitions.* Imagine working with others as capable as you at leading, who continue to develop their leadership nonnegotiables. Can you imagine how empowering and fulfilling to work in such an organization would be?

---

[8] While it's true origin is unknown, this quote is commonly attributed to the poet and author Ralph Waldo Emerson from Massachusetts during the 1800s.

Chapter 2

PERSONAL CHARACTER

This chapter will examine the first leadership nonnegotiable: personal character. We will begin with the role of personal character in leadership, followed by a review of character competencies, and finish with the importance of credibility, trust, and reputation in forming a personal character suitable for leadership. So let's get started. *Personal character* is the mental and personal qualities that make you "you." Personal character is the "**you**" you project for all to see and is influenced by your beliefs, experiences, culture, education, biases, gender, ethnicity, and so on. Being aware of how you are perceived and managing your personal character—that is, how it influences others and you—is a critical life skill and leadership nonnegotiable for two principal reasons:

> ➤ Without a relatable personal character, one's ability to lead is impaired, and
> ➤ You cannot manage or improve what you do not know.

For instance, Paul was an executive who proudly described himself as a *hothead* and wore that very apt description like a badge of honor. Regrettably, his easy-to-anger tendencies compromised his ability to lead; no one wanted to be around him. Staff and peers alike kept their distance in fear of witnessing or being the object of yet another blow-up. Paul's quick-to-anger tendencies reverberated throughout the organization; people in his division regretted coming to work and looked forward to leaving at the end of the day. Alienated from his staff and peers, Paul's executive effectiveness and position performance declined, which, in turn, increased his frustration, triggering more outbursts, and so on. Here is the point: knowing you are a hothead is one thing; caring enough to do something about it is entirely different. If personal character is not intact, no one will want to follow you. Character matters. Moreover, personal character is not something that you summon when it is time to lead and dispense with when the leadership moment passes. The "you" you project is ever-present; people know it, see it, and respond to it.

I recall being at a function that was honoring an executive for her success in growing a business (and developing its staff) from a small shop into a national presence. I was honored to be seated at her table. During our meal, someone asked her what she believed was her greatest contribution to the company's success; she replied, "Hiring good people. It is much easier to teach a good person skills, than to teach an as**ole to be a good person." Wow.

Put differently, leadership is not just the exercise of leadership knowledge; it is also tied to *who* is exercising that knowledge. The "you" you project is inescapable. Building and maintaining a suitable personal character is a prerequisite to lead. One of my favorite quotes on this topic is by Kurt Vonnegut: "We are what we pretend to be, so we must be careful about what we pretend to be." Complementing that quote is one by George Washington: "It is better to be alone than in bad company." It is no secret: a credible personal character not only allows you to fit in, but it lets you stand out when it is time to lead. It has been said that a leader should be simultaneously among and above the fray.[9] Others' perception of you as a person of character *enables* you to lead; namely, it enables you to influence others to willingly commit to a shared goal. When personal character is intact, people will not only want to be associated with you but will actively participate in helping to achieve leadership outcomes.

The point is simple: day-to-day you go about your work, home, and social life spaces being your natural, authentic self. In the conduct of being

---

[9] R. Heifitz and M. Linsky, "A survival guide for leaders," *Harvard Business Review*, June 2002.

you—the personal "you" you project—you undertake a multitude of activities and tasks to accomplish some goal or purpose. It could be a personal goal such as learning a new language, a corporate purpose such as accomplishing its mission, a family goal such as getting a pet, or a social purpose such as affiliation. If accomplishing a goal or purpose involves just you alone, then personal character has little to no influence on its outcome; however, when you need others to accomplish a goal or purpose (and vice versa), and willing cooperation, not compulsory compliance, is what you strive for, then creating and maintaining a credible personal character matters. We must be aware of the fitness of our personal character so it enables us, not limits us, to lead. The "you" you project influences mood, context, motivation, and much, much more.

More to this point: Personal character is like gravity; it keeps the "you" you project grounded (in a good way). We have all seen people who are gracious and trustworthy one minute, then leave you bleeding at the boardroom meeting the next. Supporting and friendly one moment, and then throw you under the bus the next. It is like they are on the moon— low gravity—bouncing around unable or unwilling to control or find their *character* footing. Without a sense of *character* gravity, a person is incapable of gaining the traction needed to build and sustain a meaningful personal character—daily ebbs and flows of life easily unsettle them. So find your footing; don't give anyone or anything power over the "you" you want to be (or should be).

Likely, this discussion of personal character elicits comparisons to integrity, and rightly so. Integrity is the quality of being honest and having strong moral principles. Who are you, and what do you stand for? Furthermore, personal character is reflected in how we behave. Do we conduct ourselves in a manner that is proper and expected?

Without a suitable personal character and without being seen by others as a person of integrity, influence suffocates, leaving legitimate power, coercion, manipulation, and intimidation as the remaining methods of choice to achieve a desired goal or outcome. Instead of influencing others to pursue a shared goal via commitment—a leadership outcome, use of compliance as a means of getting it done becomes the drill. A vicious cycle ensues: *poor personal character* results in loss of influence; *loss of influence* results in overreliance on legitimate power, coercion, manipulation, or intimidation; *overreliance* on compliance results in further loss of character, and so on. The very behaviors impeding leadership become the ones most reinforced.

Returning to Paul, the hotheaded executive, I was engaged by that executive's organization to conduct midlevel leadership training and executive leadership coaching for one of its divisions. Not the hotheaded executive's division, but another one. Even so, I had an opportunity to briefly talk to Paul about what I was doing, and asked him if we could have coffee or lunch to talk further. The invitation was more for me than for Paul. I wanted to understand the rationale and motivation behind his poor choice words, use of harsh tone in delivery of those words, and his generally uncivil behavior. Moreover, I wanted to get insight into what possibly the organization could have seen in Paul to promote him—and, thus, reward his behavior—to an executive position. Regardless of my intentions, in an instant, he dismissed me, saying he doesn't need or have time for that stuff, and then turned and walked away. Really? He "doesn't need or have time for that stuff"? To be sure, you cannot manage or improve what you do not know (or do not allow yourself to know). Whether it was a lack of willingness to see and/or a lack of willingness to change, the result was the same. The executive was like a bull in a china shop; he left a trail of shattered confidence and damaged relationships in his path.

It is important to realize that it is not just *what we do* and *how we do it* that projects personal character; it is also **what we say** and **how we say it**. Over time, each of us develops a personal style of communication, one that is given nuance and meaning by the "you" you project. The focus here is your *personal style of communication,* not communication styles (e.g., passive, aggressive, passive-aggressive, and open-direct). As such, it is important to know the messages and impression that your personal style of communication projects. That is, what are the descriptors (words, body language, and tone) of your personal style of communication? What messages (value for one's own needs and/or value for others' needs) does your personal style convey, and how does it impact others?

Once again, we revisit our hotheaded executive. Not only did *his choice* of words offend, but *his personal style of communicating* those words (intense eye contact, in people's face, loud-spoken, and finger-pointing) were perceived as offensive, even disrespectful. He rarely listened and had little regard for what others had to say. What staff and peers interpreted from witnessing or being the subject of one of his episodes was that work and life was all about him, and that his needs, his wants, and his interests come before those of others. The message others received was that the only person the hotheaded executive cared about and valued was himself. Though this is an extreme (though too often common) example, we need to be aware of the messages our personal style of communication conveys. An opposite example is when a person conveys high regard for others, yet little regard for himself or herself. This personal style leaves others wondering why the sender does not value himself or herself more. Healthy relationships, dialogue, leadership, and personal style require balance: seeking understanding and being understood, respecting and being respected, and valuing and being valued.

Though your personal style of communication is influenced by your background, education, experiences, etc., it does not predetermine it. You own your communication style; it is yours, and you alone are accountable for the choices you make regarding it.

CHARACTER COMPETENCIES

Knowing you (e.g., your technical competence, beliefs, and attitudes) and *managing you* (e.g., acting appropriately under pressure, managing stress, and remaining optimistic even under difficulty) are just half the challenge. Rounding out personal character includes *knowing others* (e.g., learning people's names and knowing something about each one) and *managing relationships* (e.g., considering others' feelings and accepting of differences). Why? Work (and life) takes place with people and through relationships. Mahatma Gandhi wrote: "I suppose leadership at one time meant muscles; but today it means getting along with people." How people regard and act toward others, and how others regard and act toward you, can greatly influence behavior, performance, and morale.

Therefore, leaders not only need to know and manage themselves, *personal competence (you)*, they need to be good readers of people and manage relationships, *social competence (others)*.[10] These competencies require the presence of two things: *knowing* and *managing*. You must know something before you can manage it. In other words, you cannot manage what you do not know. Therefore, *knowing you* precedes *managing you*, and *knowing others* precedes *managing relationships*. The age-old Golden Rule—do onto others how you would have them do onto you—aptly applies here. You must first be clear how you want to be treated before you can respectfully and appropriately treat others.

Before focusing on others (*knowing others* and *managing relationships*), you need to get yourself in order (*knowing you* and *managing you*). If you are out of control, then you are in no state to *know others* and *manage relationships*. Social competence requires seeking to understand others as well as being understood—*others* and *you*; balance is important. Personal and social competencies encompass the knowledge and behaviors that shape personal character, enable people to act and respond appropriately in varied environments and circumstances, and become the lenses that project the "you" that others have come to know and expect (see figure 2.1).

Figure 2.1: Personal Competence and Social Competence

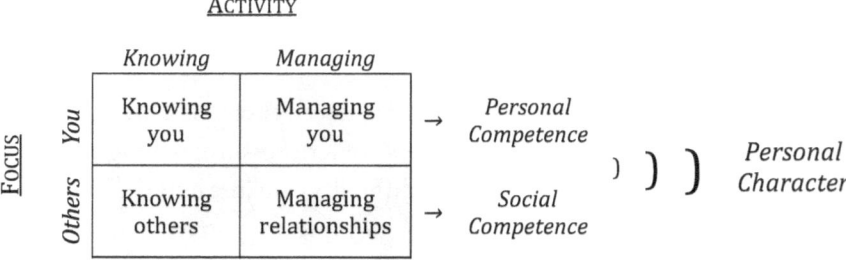

It is important to note that overemphasis or overreliance on personal or social competence can have unwelcomed outcomes. For example, overreliance on personal competence can leave a person socially inept,

---

[10] A thorough discussion of emotional intelligence competencies is presented in: D. Goleman, *Working with Emotional Intelligence* (New York: Bantam Books, 1998).

and overemphasis on social competence can cloud personal thinking and judgment. Finding and maintaining the appropriate balance, given the context, is critical. For leadership consultants or coaches, what we are discussing is known as self-monitoring behavior.[11] High self-monitors, as they are known, have the ability to regulate their behavior given the social situation.

If we assume that most people, for the most part, manage their personal character fairly well, we must still be attuned to the **blind spots** that get in the way of us seeing our true, unfiltered selves. As a result, we tend to view the world, others, and ourselves not as they and we are, but as we perceive them and us to be (or as we learned or have been taught to do so). A Stephen Covey quote is appropriate here: "We see the world, not as it is, but as we are—or, as we are conditioned to see it." Moreover, we tend to grade ourselves on a forgiving curve, while others are not so lucky. We all fall prey to the fundamental attribution error.[12] A simple example of this behavior involves you driving home after a very long day of work. You are tired. Your mind wanders. You are just not as alert as you were when you drove into work that morning. And then, someone cuts you off. Is your first thought to paint that person as not capable of driving—an idiot!? But what if you cut someone off later? Would you place the blame on your poor driving skills, or would you blame the events of the long, hard day? Perhaps, neither: it was an honest mistake caused by poor road conditions—not my fault.

Frankly, eliminating blind spots is not possible. But mitigating their effect by making oneself aware of one's blind spots or shortcomings is. To do so requires openness, courage, and, quite often, giving oneself permission to realistically assess and accept the whole of who one is—or is known/understood to be. To that end, self-assessment is helpful, and feedback can

---

[11] M. Snyder, "Self-monitoring of expressive behavior," *Journal of Personality and Social Psychology*, 1974.

[12] Simply put, the *fundamental attribution error* is the tendency for people to ascribe personality weaknesses to perceived failings of others while blaming situational circumstances to their own shortcomings. Lee Ross first coined the word in the paper "The intuitive psychologist and his shortcomings: Distortions in the attribution process," *Advances in experimental social psychology*, 1977.

be enlightening, as both can provide valuable perspectives into *personal character*. Consider this: How often are you drawn to people who tell stories of overcoming personal or professional challenges, and can express how they are all the better for the experience? Triumphs can be inspiring and motivating.

Even the very act of living exposes the *best* and *not so best* of us. We come to more fully understand our potential. Daily we are faced with the following questions:

> ➢ Am I developing those elements of my personal character that *support* desired outcomes?
> ➢ Am I willing to recognize and change (minimize or eliminate) those elements of my personal character that *detract* from desired outcomes?

It is like when you are at a social, and someone points out that piece of broccoli in your teeth.[13] You feel embarrassed. You wonder how many people saw it and said nothing. How could you get the broccoli out of your teeth if you do not know it is there? Why didn't someone say something? Did someone try to say something, and you missed it? Yes, a look in the mirror (self-assessment) or feedback can be a powerful gift—*you cannot manage or improve what you do not know.* At least now that you know, you can decide whether to do something about it.

I know an executive who has the annoying habit of checking, reading, and responding to e-mails during her own staff meetings and, frankly, everywhere, all the time (*knowing you*). Repeatedly, she would pull out her smartphone and check and respond to e-mails and messages while her staff talked to her about an important issue (*managing you*). Most people considered the repeated behavior rude and dismissive. Unfortunately, the executive was oblivious to her behavior's effect on her staff and, consequently, her behavior's impact on her and her unit's performance. Since staff felt their time and input was not valued, they were reluctant to bring anything to her attention (*knowing others*). The executive's inability

---

[13] T. S. Marshall, *Competent Leadership.*

to focus and manage workplace priorities quieted her staff; she became isolated (*managing relationships*). Sadly, the executive failed to realize that work is more than just doing the work; it is also about the people doing the work. Personal character comes with an understanding that work happens with others and through relationships.

Personal and *social competencies* are essential for building and sustaining a suitable *personal character*. Like trust, which we discuss next, it takes time to build one's personal character (as perceived by others) but it can be quickly lost. The risks and consequences of not knowing or managing us and others can be grave—what we *don't know* or *don't do* can hurt us. Moreover, we are often not a good source of information about ourselves. Sure, we know our thoughts and intentions, but we do not normally see how they translate in the eyes of others. We all have "broccoli in our teeth." If you think not, just ask someone who has frequent contact with you. They will tell you; it is there for all to see. Find it, address it (as best as you can), and stay vigilant that it does not come back.

CREDIBILITY, TRUST, AND REPUTATION

For more than a decade, I have been asking people in business, government, education, and health care what individual traits of personal character matter most in leadership. Responses have been remarkably consistent; they are:

- ➢ Credibility
- ➢ Respect
- ➢ Appreciation
- ➢ Fairness
- ➢ Confidence
- ➢ Cooperation
- ➢ Professionalism
- ➢ Trust
- ➢ Honesty
- ➢ Participation
- ➢ Open-mindedness
- ➢ Good communication
- ➢ Good listener
- ➢ Not taking things personally
- ➢ Good reputation
- ➢ Patient

Notwithstanding other factors such as the situation at hand and one's competencies and relationship networks, implicit in the above list is an understanding that the behaviors of outstanding leaders are those of outstanding people too. Within the list, three traits of personal character are overwhelming standouts: *credibility*, *trust*, and having a *good reputation*.

> ➤ Credibility: belief in what one says and does is correct and true; demonstrated expertise
> ➤ Trust: belief that one's words and actions are authentic and dependable; having confident positive expectations regarding another's conduct; having one's back
> ➤ Reputation[14]: widespread beliefs or opinions that are held regarding someone (or something)

Whose credibility, trust, and reputation are we discussing? Yours: your credibility, your trustworthiness, and your reputation. You own them. Winston Churchill was once asked if he thought that history would speak kindly of him. His immediate response was, "History will be kind to me for I intend to write it." Exactly! Our character is ours to write. If you want to be credible, then do what you must to protect your character. If you want to be trustworthy, then honor what you say you will do. If you want to have a good reputation, then, using some literary freedom of Gandhi's famous saying, "Be the *you* that you want to be."

While some traits of personal character may be considered more important than others, the whole of the list above are important mainstays of personal character. It is difficult to imagine anyone willingly following someone lacking any one of them. Not very surprising, then, *personal character* plays a critical role in being viewed as a leader and achieving leadership outcomes.

If leadership is about mobilizing people to bring about extraordinary breakthroughs in thinking and practice within organizations, then leaders are at the forefront of helping people face reality and look beyond

---

[14] Though reputation may include credibility and trust, it can encompass so much more (e.g., sense of humor, professional, respectful, confident, approachable, open-minded, and patient; as well as bully, micromanager, hypocrite, unprofessional, incompetent, intimidator, stubborn, closed-minded, arrogant, and manipulator).

the easy answers. Leaders can only do that if they themselves are willing to face reality and look beyond easy fixes with respect to their personal character.

Let's be clear: others decide your reputation and whether you are viewed as credible and trustworthy. You have little control over how others come to see you except through how you build and sustain your personal character by what you project—through commitment and consistency (in a good way). Also critical is how you relate to others (think: emotional intelligence). Since personal character is the first nonnegotiable of leadership, work on it first (see figure 2.2). Without personal character, leadership talent and management skill will do little to advance leadership outcomes. No trust, no leadership. Not credible, no one will follow you. Toxic reputation, no one will want to be near you. Remember that whatever your personal character is now, it can change (for better or worse). So get to know you, learn what you can, and apply what you learn.

Figure 2.2: Personal Character

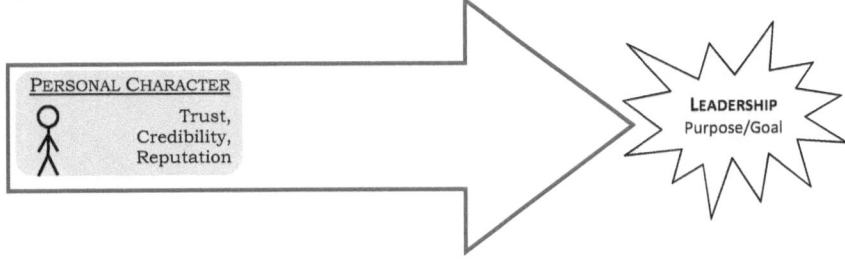

A word of caution: addressing (and thus developing) one of the leadership nonnegotiables is not accomplished at the expense of others. All three nonnegotiables must be developed and maintained in concert with one another. What good would it be if in the process of developing *leadership talent* or *management skill*, you tarnish *personal character*? None. When it comes to personal character relative to other nonnegotiables, I am reminded of the principle of triage; namely, treat the most important thing first. If personal character is lacking, work on it first. Without personal character, no one will willingly follow you. Additionally, as one seeks to develop leadership talent and management skill, he or she will learn more about himself or herself. Such insights can only enhance one's character. So keep your fingers on the pulse of personal character as you proceed, and ensure you keep what you have established. **Personal character is a precious and indispensable life and leadership commodity.**

CHAPTER 3

LEADERSHIP TALENT

"Anyone can hold the helm when the sea is calm" (Publilius Syrus). Though fluid, one's character should be consistent (in a good way). As such, one's character continues to hone and develop, especially at times when it is tested. Similarly, the second leadership nonnegotiable—*leadership talent*—should also be consistent (in a good way) and continuously nurtured and developed, and it, like character, will be tested. Who you are as a leader will be defined, in large measure, by how you lead in turbulence. In this chapter, we will examine cognitive and emotional abilities to lead, leadership styles, strategic and operational work, motivation, and assessing leadership.

The focus of leadership talent is "**people**"—you and others; this makes sense since leadership occurs within relationships (people). Likely, you have already led—or have attempted to lead—others more times than you can count whether at work or at home. Leadership applies to everyone, everywhere. It is not always planned, but when a given situation calls for leadership, someone has to step up. Leadership talent refers to the *knowledge*, *skills*, and *abilities* associated with leadership. Leadership talent also reflects a *willingness* to lead others. Furthermore, and let's be clear: leadership is not about a position one holds. Leadership is not tied to one's place in the organizational hierarchy or one's title. John C. Maxwell, an American author, speaker, and pastor, wrote: "Leadership is not about titles, positions, or flowcharts. It is about one's life influencing another."

Over the years, I have been fortunate to witness impressive leadership by people who have a title or position, but the more compelling examples of leadership that I have seen are by those individuals recognized as leaders by their peers but who do not have title or occupy a "leadership" position. Such individuals reflect authentic leadership. Overwhelmingly it is true, leadership is not based upon where you sit; it is about what you do when called upon.

Two conditions must be present for leadership talent to exist:

> ➤ Integrated cognitive and emotional abilities to lead: have the *knowledge, skills, ability,* and *confidence* to lead, and
> ➤ Motivation to lead: have the *willingness* to lead.

For example, a person may desperately want to lead but not know how, and a person may know how to lead but does not want to. Different conditions require different treatments. In both cases, leadership and leadership outcomes may suffer. To reiterate, occupying an executive, managerial, or supervisory position does not make one a leader—such positions are not synonymous with leadership. Moreover, it is important to keep in mind that leadership is inherently about partnerships. Leaders partner with those who will join with them to accomplish a desired outcome. Leaders also partner with one another to accentuate the talents of each other while eliminating any inherent weaknesses.

INTEGRATED COGNITIVE AND EMOTIONAL ABILITIES TO LEAD

As noted in chapter 1, to effectively lead requires balanced cognitive and emotional abilities, as it is the presence of both that enables each of us to navigate opportunities and challenges. Leaders must be good readers of people and able to customize leadership styles to meet specific individual and/or group needs. The "readers of people" comes from the social competency of personal character. The "you" that becomes evident through personal character can be further portrayed via common styles inherent to leaders. It is important to understand that these leadership styles complement and accentuate personal character (and vice versa). Without a suitable personal character, leadership ability is compromised and achievements (e.g., outcomes from the exercise of leadership) will likely suffer as a result. What does this mean? It means if personal character is lacking, then personal character must be acquired (or restored) first. Personal character is a prerequisite to leadership talent—a leadership *a priori*. Once present, while continuing to monitor and maintain personal character, go to work on developing leadership ability (talent). Attention to both is concurrent and ever present.

It is through the application and customization of these styles that we, as leaders, meet specific individual, team, and/or organization needs. To do so requires understanding each style and its use, and, more importantly, its relationship with the other styles.[15] A brief description of each leadership style follows:

➢ Work-Focused: Has high standards and a strong drive for achievement. Such an individual is performance driven, consistently maintains high levels of production, painstakingly monitors performance, and works with vigor, effectiveness, and determination.

➢ People-Focused: Promotes harmony, unity, and builds constructive relationships. Such an individual relieves stress, recognizes the emotional needs of others, behaves professionally and supportively to create mutual goals, and minimizes conflict.

➢ Commanding/Decisive: Provides structure, rigid controls, and issues instructions without necessarily asking for input. Such an individual exudes confidence but may have an intimidating demeanor and may not be a good listener.

➢ Listener/Collaborator: Is a superb listener, collaborator, and influencer. Such an individual persists in seeking understanding

---

[15] Adapted from multiple sources: D. Goleman, R. Boyatzis, and A. McKee, *Primal Leadership: Unleashing the Power of Emotional Intelligence,* (Cambridge, MA: Harvard Business Review Press, 2013); and P. Hershey, K. H. Blanchard, and D. E. Johnson, *Management of Organizational Behavior: Leading Human Resources,* 10th ed. (Upper Saddle River, NJ: Pearson, 2012).

despite difficulties; responds to comments (good and bad) in a way that reflects understanding; and values peoples' input and gains buy-in.

➢ Coach/Mentor: Focuses on nurturing, developing, and motivating others. Such an individual builds knowledge, skills, abilities, and the confidence to do so effectively by providing challenging assignments to develop both capability and confidence.

➢ Visionary/Dreamer: Visionary leaders provide a sense of purpose and focus. Such an individual can *see clarity in chaos* as well as *articulate the way forward*; and as a result, people are drawn not only to him or her but to his or her vision.

The six leadership styles presented in figures 3.1 and 3.3 represent **vertical** and **horizontal relationships**, respectively, among different, yet complementary leadership styles. Let's first consider the vertical relationships of the leadership styles.

LEADERSHIP STYLES—VERTICAL RELATIONSHIPS

The connection between *work-focused* and *people-focused* styles is obvious: it is **focus**. These two styles acknowledge that leaders do more than just ensure work gets done—*work-focused*, they also need to know about the people doing the work—*people-focused*. Style extremes range from "*kumbaya*" to "*you have a job to do, do your job.*" For instance, suppose you assumed the lead of a team that has suffered for months under an extreme workload; though the bulk of the work has passed, morale is low. Well, taking the time to recognize the team's sacrifices and honor their commitment would be wise—*people-focused*; once revitalized, refocus their attentions and energies on accomplishing the team's purpose/goal—*work-focused*. Alternatively, what if you inherited a team that has been too *people-focused* at the expense of actually getting real work done? Here, one would need to direct efforts to completing the work while retaining the requisite harmony and unity.

Figure 3.1: Leadership Styles—Vertical Relationships

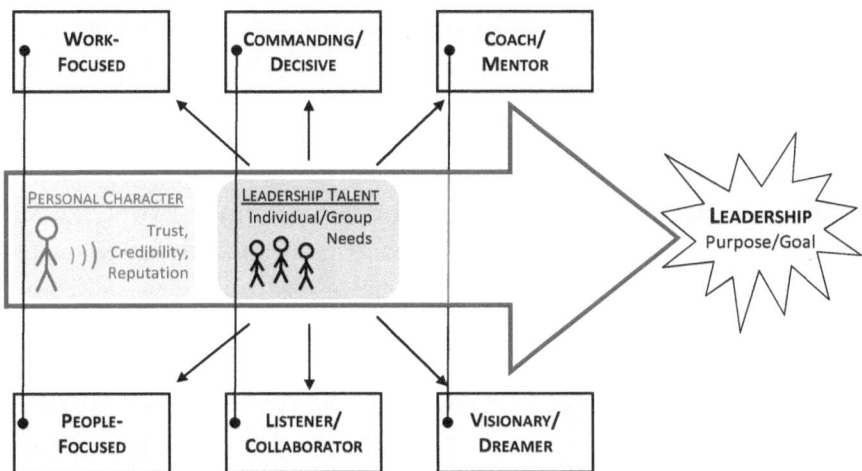

Commanding/decisive and *listener/collaborator* leadership styles likewise are different, yet complementary. While the *commanding/decisive* style advocates and asserts, the *listener/collaborator* style includes and collaborates—**time** is a major consideration here. Style extremes here range from *"No discussion, just do it"* to *"What do you think? Let's talk."*

You may find the *commanding/decisive* leadership style not to be a very good listener. Why is that so? Well, there is no time for talk—urgency for action is needed now. Alternatively, a *listener/collaborator* leadership style likely has the luxury of time to listen carefully and seek input. Consider the following example: suppose your unit just got an urgent assignment from the agency head with instructions to drop everything else. What is needed is decisive, commanding direction to accomplish an urgent task; given the situation, forming a committee and seeking extensive input would be ill advised—there is no time.

Accordingly, it is important to find balance between these two styles. Some people cannot do anything until they know everything; result: nothing gets done. We know these types, and all we want is for them to make a decision. However, there are others who make hasty decisions without knowing what they are deciding; result: direct, upstream and downstream consequences abound. Bottom line: leaders must be good readers of people and environments, and lead appropriately. Sometimes, things need to be slowed down to allow for discussion and collaboration; other times, sped up requiring directness and decisiveness.

Finally, though *coach/mentor* and *visionary/dreamer* leadership styles approach work differently, both styles are vital for the successful completion of anything. **Approach** is a chief consideration with these two styles. The *visionary/dreamer* style is unbound by constraints and able to see the big picture, taking a strategic approach; thus, he or she is able to provide clarity in chaos as well as articulate the way forward. The *coach/mentor* style takes an operational approach, and builds knowledge, skills, abilities, and the confidence not only to do a job but to do it well. These styles complement one another—one is able to see and articulate the future; the other makes it happen. What one style *envisions*: where are we going and why; the other *describes*: explains how we will get there.

Visionary/dreamer and coach/mentor leadership styles, as well as innovator and entrepreneur approaches, reside in strategic and operational work (see figure 3.2). For example, *strategic work* belongs to the visionary/ dreamer (innovator) who imagines new futures and new products/ services, respectively. Likewise, *operational work* belongs to the coach/ mentor (entrepreneur) who develops people, and develops and delivers things, respectively. Successful performance requires both. Yet, in many situations, it is a tall order to expect one individual to be skilled in both style competencies. Instead of thinking that one leader can (and should) do it all, we should remember that multiple individuals talented with respect to strategic and operational work can work and lead together.

Figure 3.2: Strategic and Operational Work

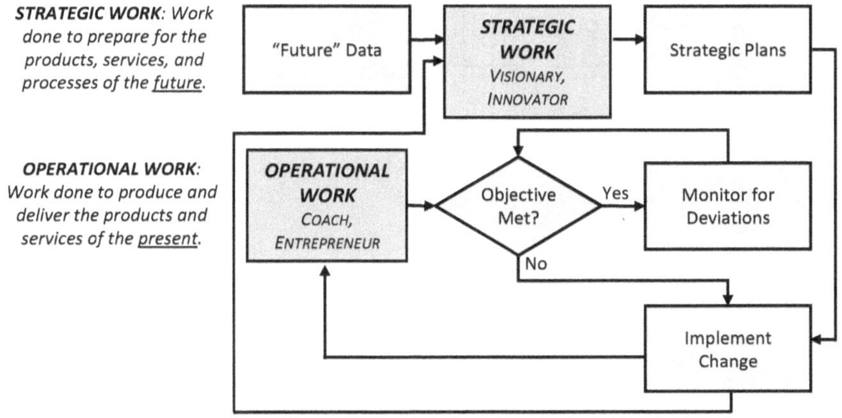

STRATEGIC WORK: Work done to prepare for the products, services, and processes of the *future*.

"Future" Data

STRATEGIC WORK
VISIONARY, INNOVATOR

Strategic Plans

OPERATIONAL WORK: Work done to produce and deliver the products and services of the *present*.

OPERATIONAL WORK
COACH, ENTREPRENEUR

Objective Met? — Yes — Monitor for Deviations

No

Implement Change

LEADERSHIP STYLES—HORIZONTAL RELATIONSHIPS

Just as there are vertical leadership style relationships (e.g., *people-focused* and *work-focused* styles), so, too, are there **horizontal leadership style relationships** (e.g., *work-focused, commanding/decisive,* and *coach/mentor*)—see figure 3.3. For example, suppose a unit is not performing well; employees seem competent, but the previous team lead let them get away with poor performance. What is needed is some straight talk and tough love; namely, decisive direction about getting things done (*commanding/decisive*) coupled with milestones and challenging goals that provide performance monitoring (*work-focused*) supported by feedback and confidence building (*coach/mentor*) to get performance back on track. In many ways, the horizontal relationships of *work-focused, commanding/decisive,* and *coach/mentor* together reflect expectations we hold for managers while those *people-focused, listener/collaborator,* and *visionary/dreamer* individuals signal traditional leadership qualities. Again, it is important to remember that teams and organizations require both leadership talent (leaders) and management skill (leaders who can manage—or who finds others who can). It is hard to separate the two, nor should we. Keeping in mind how the styles complement each other (as discussed in chapter 1), in a given situation, is key.

Figure 3.3: Leadership Styles—Horizontal Relationships

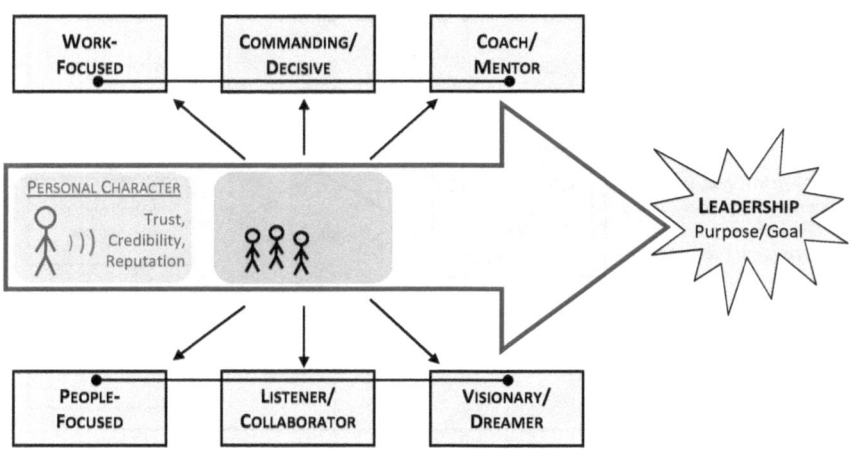

Vertical and horizontal mismatches are possible, but unusual. For example, if your mission has just shifted, and you have to change the way you have been doing your work, then what is needed, at least initially, is a *visionary/ dreamer* leader to provide focus and a clear vision that demonstrates how previous skill sets will fit into the new mission. This style would likely be aligned with inclusion and collaboration (*listener/collaborative*) as well as strategies to lessen the stress brought on by the mission shift (*people-focused*). What is unlikely in this example—that is, out of alignment—would be issuing instructions without asking for input (*commanding/decisive*) and painstakingly monitoring performance (*work-focused*). Such actions would likely stifle resilience, dampen morale, and stall performance.

Finally, delivery of leadership styles must be authentic—reinforced continuously through *words*, *tone*, and *body language*. If all three aspects of communication fail to convey a coherent message, then leadership outcomes may suffer. Regardless of your personal style of communication or personality styles (introvert or extravert), leaders must either have mastery of delivery of all six leadership styles or partner with other talented individuals who do. Leading appropriately requires credible, capable, and competent leadership—the leadership nonnegotiables; these nonnegotiables blend personal and social competencies with organizational purpose and priorities to achieve leadership outcomes.

Suppose the tall stick figure under "Personal Character" is you (figure 3.3), and you are the team lead for the three smaller stick figures under "Leadership Talent." Day-to-day, everyone (including you) is going about his or her day focused on accomplishing the mission of the team. At that moment, no leadership style(s) is in direct play; we are all just going about our work being our natural selves. Then a crisis resulting from an external or internal cause erupts affecting the team; mission focus gets disrupted. It would be appropriate for the team lead, *you*, to respond in a suitable manner to address the situation and refocus the team on their mission. But keep in mind that leading does not always mean taking direct charge; sometimes the best leaders allow others to step forward—integrating, nurturing, and mentoring the leadership talents of others. A Lao Tao quote is suitable here: "When the best leader's work is done the people say, 'We did it ourselves.'" In other words, the "designated" (or "expected") leader is willing to be led.

MOTIVATION TO LEAD

In addition to being a good reader of people, leaders must be good readers of environments and understand how varying contexts and situations influence motivation, including their own. Like reading people, reading environments is a competency; so, like before, we will concentrate on enhancing our understanding of motivation.

Motivation is the driving reason for *willing action* and ideally comes from within us. Let us start with "willing action." Yes, you can force movement or compliance through legitimate power, manipulation, coercion, or intimidation, but that is not willing action, nor motivation—it is power (personal or position). Willing action comes from fulfilling a compelling reason(s) to act, move, or commit. Fulfillment of needs, ambitions, etc., is what motivates most of us. To that end, in order to motivate someone, you have to know *what* motivates them—needs, interests, desires, goals, etc.—before you can know *how* to motivate them. Knowing the *what* leads to the *how*. That being the case, it is incumbent for leaders to create an environment that encourages and enables motivation to grow and flourish. Leaders do not move people; they influence movement.

Compelling reasons that motivate are recognition, responsibility, achievement, challenge, and growth. As opposed to extrinsic rewards, these compelling reasons reflect intrinsic motivation. If leadership is one of the most studied business topics by sheer volume of books written, how to motivate people is not far behind. David McClelland's seminal human motivation theory[16] explains how needs for achievement, affiliation, and power affect behavior in organizations. If a person has a strong need to belong, then create an environment that enables collaboration and teamwork. If achievement is the need, then structure work for them to make presentations, write procedures, or manage supplies. If it is position, then help them meet their needs by leading meetings, chairing committees, or making decisions that affect others.

McClelland, along with David Burnham, also studied the motivations of effective leaders.[17] Leaders are not immune to needs for achievement, affiliation, and power. Yet, what separated successful leaders from those less successful leaders was a high need for power, but not power in its usual form (e.g., to get someone to do something they wouldn't otherwise do). Instead, the high power motivation was balanced by high inhibition. High inhibition is represented by greater concern for others and the organization, over personal gain. Such leaders exhibited *socialized power* in which the use of power was altruistic. As a leader, what could be more indicative of authenticity than working for and with others?

---

[16] McClelland discussed affiliation, achievement, and power as motivators to performance. More can be learned from: D. C. McClelland, *The Achieving Society* (New York: Free Press, 1961).
[17] D. C. McClelland and D. H. Burnham, "Power is the great motivator," *Harvard Business Review*, January 2003.

ASSESSING LEADERSHIP

Before considering the third leadership nonnegotiable—management skill, presented in the next chapter—assessing leadership style strengths can give insight into how one can improve upon the competency and exercise of leadership. Figure 3.4 below illustrates results and feedback from a leadership style assessment. Note: The leadership assessment shown below is not a substitute for other highly valuable assessments (e.g., Myers-Briggs Type Indicator, Emotional Intelligence, 360° assessments); rather, it is a quick and useful method for existing and emerging leaders to self-assess leadership talent and leadership inclinations/opportunities.

Figure 3.4: Leadership Styles Assessment and Feedback

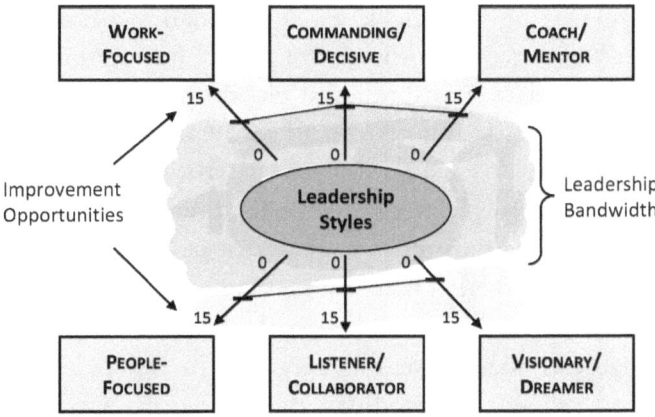

Assessment ratings are indicated by the hash marks (-) across vertical lines. Shown in the diagram above, the area between the ratings (0 rating to a given hash mark) indicates leadership bandwidth; the areas outside the hash marks (from the hash mark to 15 rating) represent opportunities for improvement (see figure 3.4). The leadership style assessment becomes even more useful when it is accompanied with ratings from one's own supervisor, peers, and direct reports. See appendix 1 for a shortened leadership assessment.

CHAPTER 4

MANAGEMENT SKILL

The third nonnegotiable of leadership is *management skill*. Its focus is **"things"**—*you manage things*. In this chapter, we will discuss staffing, budgeting, managing with data, and performance measures. Though leaders must have a working knowledge of core management skills (e.g., staffing, budgets, data, measures, and planning), execution of them is frequently a collaborative effort with subject matter experts. Supporting these management skills is a host of other activities such as prioritizing, scheduling, problem solving, and decision making. Let's state the obvious: in work (as in life), there are often far more things to do than we have time to do them. As such, there is not now, nor will there ever be, enough time for leaders to focus on all relevant issues. There are just too many issues—longstanding, recent, and as-yet-to-emerge—to attend to. Needless to say, a leader's most valuable commodity is time. If one cannot manage his or her time, then his or her ability to lead people and manage things—the focus of this chapter—is severely diminished.

Broadly speaking, management skill requires understanding the integrated system of service, production, and delivery that supports organizational performance; it includes people (in a staffing context) and other things. Even if personal character and leadership talent are flawless, if you do not also manage well, performance may suffer. Thus, the best leaders either possess such management skills, or they surround themselves with people who do. This chapter is going to review four interdependent management skills that are vital to the success of any business, organization, division, team, etc. The four skills are: staffing, budgeting, managing with data, and performance measures (see figure 4.1). A fifth essential management skill, strategic planning, is presented in chapter 5; and a sixth, implementing change, is presented in chapter 6.

Figure 4.1: Management Skill

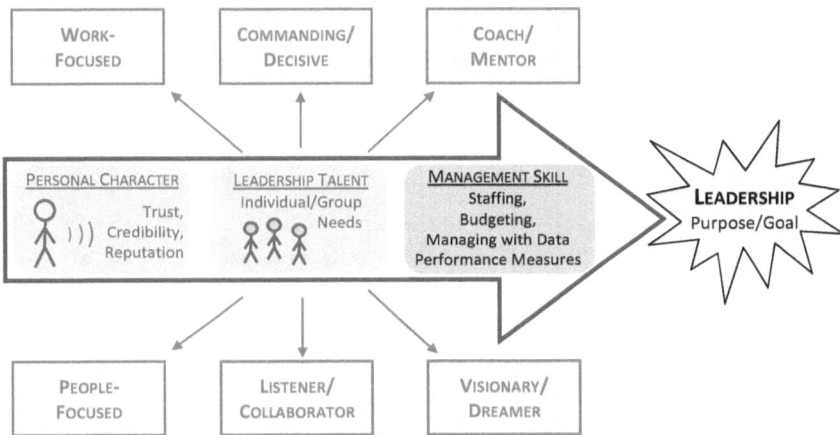

All these management skills are interdependent because the successful execution of any one requires the existence of the others (as mentioned above). For example, staffing requires budgeting—you have to pay for what you get; staffing and budgeting require data (information)—how many staff at what skill levels and at what cost; and staffing, budgeting, and managing with data are dependent on meaningful performance measures/measurements. Finally, "Strategic Planning," chapter 5, and "Implementing Change," chapter 6, rely on all the above for successful planning and execution.

STAFFING

Staffing (people management) is a critical skill that a leader must grasp. People management includes the planning and deployment of people (quantity and quality) and positions (numbers and types) to ensure the efficient and effective distribution of talent through a team, unit, or organization. Staffing an organization is not a static affair, and consequently, it involves on-going recruitment, hiring, and succession planning. Though the human resource management (HRM) shop plays a significant staffing role, leaders must understand enough of the basics in order to intelligently collaborate with and meaningfully advise HRM professionals on the various roles and assignments needed to conduct business (now and in the future).

Staffing comprises both a supply and a demand side. The activity of hiring and training people (supply) to meet an organization's talent needs (demand) today and three to five years out (strategic planning) is no easy endeavor. Staffing remains a moving target. The reality is, every executive, manager, and employee will eventually leave the unit, division, and organization. Turnover is a fact of organizational life. With each departure, not only does the person go, but he or she takes with him or her the knowledge, competencies, and experiences that fueled organizational performance. Also, key relationships end, affecting fellow employees and customers.

People management provides the staffing framework, talent development, and onboarding pipeline to ensure that existing talent stays current and that emerging talent is ready to assume key positions when the need arises. Every movement on the diagram below (see figure 4.2) is driven and guided by a well-thought-out staffing, talent management, and succession plan.

Figure 4.2: Staffing, Talent Management, and Succession Planning

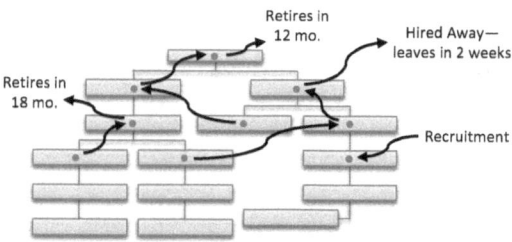

When people management and planning are done well, they provide talent continuity, build bench strength, and assure the availability and readiness of talent to assume existing and future organizational roles. Ask any leader: "What is your most valuable asset?" The answer is invariably "people." If true, significant business shifts are not the biggest hurdle to overcome on a daily basis. Instead, the challenge is the day-to-day management of people, including keeping the people motivated. Yet, an unfortunate truth is the answer to the following question: *How much time do leaders spend on staffing plans?* The likely answers are: "not much" or "not as much as they would like." While some leaders may be resistant or do not see the need to develop (and update) staffing plans, the majority simply do not dedicate the necessary time to people management. Remember that time is always in short supply. If people are a priority, then *the best leaders make time for people.*

The rationale for succession planning and talent management is simply based on the odds of finding and recruiting the right person, with the right skills, at just the right time for a specific position. The odds are low. Perfect matches rarely occur. Besides, such a focus is solely on hiring, not the development of people over time. Anticipating personnel changes (succession planning) and grooming talent (talent management) to assume key roles when needed is a reasonable strategy—not in lieu of other methods (e.g., recruiting), but in conjunction with them.

Keep in mind, the goal of staffing is not to maintain or replace incumbents with people exactly like them. Changes in strategic plans, goals, and priorities must be considered to make sure that incumbent competencies or replacements have the knowledge, skills, abilities, behaviors, and other characteristics to perform the jobs and work roles of the future successfully— those needed to move the organization forward. Key staffing questions include: Are staff levels and staffing decisions consistent with workplace demands (present and projected)? Do staffing practices (numbers, skills, and experience) support performance—present and future? Are staffing expectations changing? Does the organization have the right levels and mix of talent to support effectiveness and its competitive advantage?

Granted, there is a very good chance that significant organizational shifts will influence staffing and succession plans, just as they will likely influence strategic planning and strategic plans, budgetary planning and budgets, and so on. That is a good thing. All planning processes, including staff planning, should be ongoing, fluid, and adaptable. When it comes to staffing an organization, there is no such thing as perfection.

In closing, while staffing a unit or organization seems very logical, quite desirable, and imminently possible, in practice, the process takes a great deal of communication, cooperation, hard work, and, of course, patience and discipline from all parties involved. That being said, it is better to have a less-than-perfect staffing plan—at least initially—than no plan at all.

BUDGETING

Budgeting, especially the types and the complexities of organizational budgets, can be overwhelming. Unless you are educated in the *whys* (reasons) and *wherefores* (how it came to be) underlying budgets and experienced in your organization's budgeting process, it is usually best to leave sophisticated budgets and budgeting to the experts. Even so, leaders must have a working knowledge of how budgets translate into product and service delivery, and vice versa. At a minimum, leaders should have a good understanding of the mechanics of budgeting, recognize that resources are scarce, that there is competition for resources, and have a deep appreciation for budgetary measurement, performance, and accountability. At the center of all budgeting is the need to be able to quantify cost, revenue, and outcomes.

In regard to budgets, leaders struggle daily with the importance of identifying priorities and allocating scarce resources to meet those priorities. Those activities that can be easily monetized (e.g., the benefits exceed costs) will invariably be viewed more positively and get attention (e.g., funded) first. Further complicating the budgeting process is the reality of stakeholders, executives, and others throwing their political weight around to get what they want. As a result, leaders must frequently juggle scarce dollars to secure in-demand resources. At best, budgets are based upon assumptions and predictions—an inexact science. Specifically, a budget is a *forecast* of the need (demand) for a product, service, or information, and the available resources (supply) to deliver that product, service, or information for a given time period. Budgets set targets, targets that are used later to assess performance.

As part of the budgeting process, leaders frequently look at alternative means of addressing specific product and service delivery costs, including contracting out, replacement costs, or even relying on a different strategy to respond to changing situations. To reasonably estimate (forecast) future costs, you need to consider seasonal and month-to-month cost variations, causes of cost fluctuations, anticipate rate adjustments, and more. As you can imagine, communication during budget development and implementation is critical. And, budgets are never static. As business conditions shift, budgets are adjusted.

Consider a household budget. It is normally developed by considering income and *mandatory* (e.g., housing, food, clothing, transportation, etc.) and *discretionary* (e.g., vacations, entertainment, savings, etc.) spending. In developing household budgets, individuals often consider such *policy* factors as a desire to move into a larger home, a desire for a better car, or to set funds aside to accommodate unexpected expenses. Additionally, family size and the ages of children, a desire for a more comfortable lifestyle, and other factors can impact year-to-year changes in a household budget. There is plenty of politicking as well. Whether it is at work or at home, the budget should be developed and displayed in a fashion that makes it *easily understood* by everyone, yet has sufficient information to justify the requested level of funding. Ultimately, people will dissect the numbers to get to, "Did what I want get funded?" *Justification* of *wants* can be an art form. You may want a new Maserati, but in the end the need—an economy vehicle suited for transportation purposes—will win out.

Though perhaps unnecessary to say, remember that the only certainty in budgeting is uncertainty. Budgets reflect assumptions made at a given point in time. Once in place and with the passage of time, each assumption is validated or exposed as overly optimistic or overly conservative. Tips for living and surviving with budgeting uncertainty are: frequent communication, do not lose sight of the mission, focus on expected outcomes, and, before any budgeting deficiencies are uncovered, have an adjustment strategy in place. The ability to adjust begins with scenario planning. From the outset of budget season, organizations build multiple budgets based on potential deviations in revenues and/or expenses. Consequently, when budget season arrives, it is all about one's *preparation* with respect to his or her ability to defend what is needed, regardless of the scenario. Preparation depends on having the information (e.g., the facts, the data) to defend one's position.

MANAGING WITH DATA

Every day people use numerical data to successfully navigate life's activities and challenges. We check time of day, monitor speed, count calories and steps, check bank balances, cook at specified temperatures and times, meet at certain times and lengths, and on and on. It is the presence of numerical data that allows us to plan, manage, and coordinate activities sensibly. Could you imagine setting your sights on a goal without knowing if you had the means (e.g., time and resources) to get there? You would not. Managing in the absence of data would be very shortsighted.

It is the presence of numerical data that helps us manage and minimize risks, uncertainties, and consequences. Think of the chance (*risk*) of getting a ticket when driving with an inaccurate or inoperative speedometer (*uncertainty, no reliable data*). Such an act may cause dire *consequences*—speeding ticket, an appearance in court, increased insurance rates. Likewise, consider a speedometer that is *accurate*, but not *timely*—only updates speed every five minutes. Oh my! Given the circumstances, establishing appropriate data requirements are critical. So managing with timely, reliable, numerical data is essential to day-to-day living (at work and at home); it enhances decision making. In other words, information in context yields knowledge, and (timely) knowledge improves decision making.

While managing with data is an essential and common practice for most people at home, that sound practice too often is not carried into the workplace. Far too many people can argue that many significant mission, program, and resource decisions have been shaped by or based upon opinions, anecdotes, wishes, and hopes of what one would *like* to happen, rather than on what is *realistic* and, thus, based on meaningful numerical data. Decisions that we would cringe to make at home involving a fraction of the resource, we readily make at work without a second thought. Perhaps it is because the workplace makes some feel insulated from the consequences of their decisions. Whatever the reason, failing to manage with meaningful, timely, numerical performance information can be costly. It can rob organizations, staff, and stakeholders of management trust, confidence, and ability.

The premise is simply this: successful people and organizations use numerical data to manage and communicate performance. They do not rely upon anecdotes, rumors, gossip, wishes, hopes, or guesses to make important decisions. Though many organizations have adopted a practice of measuring and reporting, few use numerical data effectively to drive performance and thus accountability. While well intended, *measuring and reporting are often disconnected* (vertically and horizontally) from the results that organizations, stakeholders, and customers need, let alone want. The following tends to be a reliable set of questions in this regard: *Why* is the data needed? *Who* will collect the data? *What* data will be collected? *When* will the data be collected? *Where* will the data be collected? *How much* data will be needed? *How often* will the data be collected? *How long* will the data be collected? *How* will the data be recorded and organized?

The effectiveness of leaders is compromised when they are not actively engaged in deciding *what* is measured, *how* it is measured, and then *how* it is reported. Too often in organizations, failure to sequence and align the *whats* and *hows* can have dire consequences resulting in the all-too-common complaints of having not measured the right thing or having measured the right thing but in the wrong way—of which neither may have arrived in time to render a proper decision. Ultimately, what is reported is virtually useless. This is what is known as a perpetual, suboptimizing loop of *never having the right data at the right time in the right format*. It is little wonder why executives, employees, customers, and other stakeholders are left wondering why things are not getting better, when decisions are based on flawed performance indicators.

It is through a commitment to measurement that organizations can assess how value is created (and how value is being leeched away). For organizations to achieve the best possible results, measuring and reporting must be interdependent functions that support making decisions. In addition, leaders must move beyond using measures merely to manage and report how things are (*current performance*); they must steadfastly resolve to provide seasoned analysis that provides insight into where they should be (*desired performance*), as well as what needs to be maintained, improved, or abandoned.

Leaders must outline what matters and then ensure it gets measured. They need measures that help them allocate, align, and focus resources on what is important, not just what is urgent. Finally, organizations must use meaningful measures and prepare useful reports that help lines-of-business achieve results, enhance trust, restore confidence, improve management, show accountability, demonstrate performance, and, most importantly, improve performance. If done right, managing with data can help organizations align efforts and resources (inputs) to produce value-added products and services (outputs) that will more likely achieve desired results (outcomes).

As noted with respect to staffing and budgeting, there needs to be a plan. And plans take time to develop. First and foremost, doing it right requires knowing what you need (and want) to know. Credibly answering what you need to know requires meaningful measures of performance, reliable data collection, appropriate analysis, interpretation in context, and a means of conveying the results. Finally, doing it right requires management action and follow-up. If you do not know what you want to know, then pause data collection until you do. Chasing data beforehand often ends in expended effort with little results. Consider the following:

> ➢ *If you know what you need to know*, but poorly manage the data, what follows—desired results—may suffer.
> ➢ *If you know what you need to know, expertly manage the data*, but poorly convey performance information, the story can get lost, and what follows may suffer.
> ➢ *If you know what you need to know, expertly manage the data, and convincingly convey performance information*, but take no action, it can result in a regretful waste of resources, low morale, and loss of management confidence.
> ➢ Finally, *if you know what you need to know, expertly manage the data, convincingly convey performance information, and take action*, but no one follows up to see the action through, what could have been may never be.

So, when it comes to managing with data (see appendix 2), one cannot cut corners. Getting quality performance information is hard work. That is probably why many leaders go straight from situation to decision with only a glance at the available data. Taking the easy route is a recipe for disaster. Frankly, anyone can make decisions, but making credible decisions requires a solid understanding of the role, purpose, use, and limitations of performance information in decision making and, ultimately, in management, planning, and accountability. *Leader competence in this area is essential for organizations to succeed; it is not an optional skill set.* Like other management skills, leaders do not have to manage data on their own; if in doubt, get help. Many organizations have performance data experts (or retain consultants) who can provide guidance.

Such guidance includes *understanding what cannot be measured and why*. Consider that the more complex the situation, the greater the uncertainty, the greater the associated risk, and, very likely, the greater the need for credible, not anecdotal, information. However, the more complex the situation, the greater the likelihood there will be gaps in what data can be provided. Alternatively, guidance comes from *establishing lead and lag measures*.[18] Lead measures are key improvement indicators and track actions being undertaken. Lag measures reflect desired future (lag) goals. For example, we would track the frequency of brushing one's teeth (a lead measure) before measuring the number of (decrease in) cavities (a lag measure).

The purpose of managing with data—meaning having the best possible information available—is to gain insight, understanding, and knowledge into the performance of key organization processes, activities, and issues. Performance data serves as a powerful *complement* to a person's knowledge, judgment, and experience; *it is not a substitute for it*. Essentially, given (within reason) what time will allow, more credible information is better than less when it comes to decision quality. If information gaps exist, do not succumb to routine. Instead, continue to improve upon how information is collected, analyzed, and reported. Organizations must evaluate how they measure with data.

---

[18] See C. McChesney, S. Covey, and J. Huling, *The 4 Disciplines of Execution: Achieving Your Wildly Important Goals* (New York: Free Press, 2012).

Broadly speaking, use of numerical data works like this: *meaningful measures* provide insight into organizational performance, this *insight* enhances decision making, *better decision making* fosters performance, and *improved performance* generates *better results* (and improved measurement plans). Remember improved performance creates (or restores) business trust, value, and confidence.

DEVELOPING AND USING PERFORMANCE MEASURES

Since most of this chapter involves measuring the performance of something (e.g., staffing, budgeting, processes, systems) in order to enhance its outcome, concluding the chapter with a discussion of performance measures seems appropriate. So let's begin with the definition, purpose, and use of performance measures:

> ➢ Definition: A performance measure yields a quantifiable indicator that documents change in a specific condition or attribute (e.g., staff hours, revenue).[19]
> ➢ Purpose: A performance measure is used to measure and monitor the behavior of a key characteristic, property, or attribute—is it getting better, worse, or staying the same?
> ➢ Use: A key reason to use performance measures is to meaningfully assess current performance and reasonably anticipate future performance to enhance decision making.

In so many areas, leadership (and management) success is grounded in the understanding and use of numerical data; that is because it is the presence of numerical data that leads to insight, understanding, and knowledge of the performance of key processes, activities, and issues. That knowledge is then used to enhance decision making, strategic planning, budgeting,

---

[19] The terms *measure* and *metric* are informally used interchangeably; however, *measure* is commonly used to describe objective, quantitative data, and *metric* is commonly used to describe subjective, qualitative data. Though objective, quantitative data is a preferred, we understand that not all key data elements may be quantitative. In such cases, quantifying qualitative data becomes necessary. While the process to do this is well-known and understood, discussion is beyond the scope of this book.

staffing, and much more. Most importantly, performance measures are a powerful complement to one's knowledge, judgment, and experience, not a substitute for it.

Could you image receiving a physical without it being supported by numerical data; instead you are told: "You look healthy. See you next year." Never! Exam credibility comes from careful use, examination, and review (in context) of numerical indicators of physical health (e.g., heart rate, blood pressure, cholesterol, blood sugar, weight). The presence of reliable performance data enhances a leader's judgment and decision making. Would you invest in stocks or property without knowing anything about it? Of course not; such a behavior would be ill-advised, careless, and risky. Ditto to organizational applications.

A high-level overview of the process of developing performance measures—illustrated in six steps—is provided in appendix 2. This overview assumes an entity (e.g., an organization, division, team from any given sector) has defined *where it is*, *where it wants to be*, and *how it is going to get there*; in other words, has a strategic plan (discussed in the next chapter). A chief aim of developing a portfolio of meaningful measures is to align performance toward a common aim. In the absence of a strategic plan, the development of measures can still occur; however, it will just require considerably more coordination and cooperation to ensure measures align to a common purpose now and in the future. Again, there are specialists trained in the collection and presentation of data.

CHAPTER 5

STRATEGIC PLANNING

The previous three chapters presented the three leadership nonnegotiables in isolation. Yet, as has been emphasized throughout this book, success at leading occurs when the three nonnegotiables are integrated to bring people together to accomplish *something* important. Within organizations, two of the most vital *somethings* are the creation of a strategic plan and the implementation of change. Leaders are essential to strategy formation, implementation, and organizational change. Strategic planning (see figure 5.1), an essential leadership nonnegotiable, is discussed in this chapter.

Figure 5.1: Toward a Strategic Plan

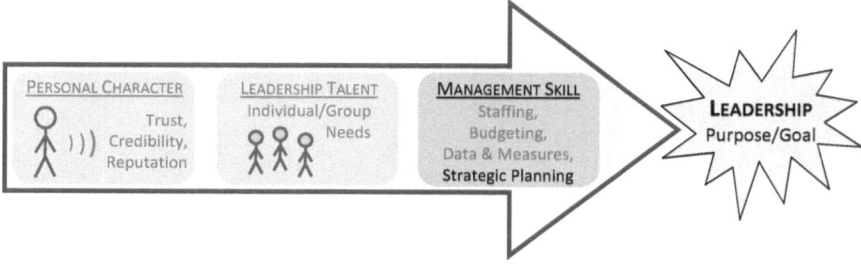

In the early 1960s, Alfred Chandler defined strategy as the determination of the basic long-term goals and objectives of an enterprise, and the adoption of courses of action and the allocation of resources for carrying out those goals and objectives. Note the definition reflects the *formation* of strategy and the *implementation* of strategy. Yet, in the heat of the moment, leaders and stakeholders can clamor for "a plan" as though it was a takeout meal. As a result, staffers/planners get caught up in the urgency of having a strategic plan and begin working on it before fully understanding the process. Production (formation) of a strategic plan, not the execution (implementation) of it, is seen as the end-state. Nothing could be further from the truth. Hastily created plans typically lack meaningful assessments of *where we are* and provide an unrealistic picture of *where we are going*. Moreover, some make strategic planning out to be rocket science, but it does not have to be. Still, creating a meaningful, deployable strategic plan does take time and discipline if it is going to have any lasting (and meaningful) impact. To realize the potential of a strategic plan, implementation is the key. There are far too many examples of strategic plans that have been developed and codified on paper (or as an electronic document) only to be tucked away in a file.

STRATEGIC PLANNING OVERVIEW AND FRAMEWORK

Strategic planning is not static, and its development and implementation reflects an adaptive process of fit[20]: internal fit (alignment with strategy and structure), external fit (alignment of strategy and environment), and dynamic fit (maintenance of internal and external fit over time). As we can speak of managing or leading, we can also speak of strategizing. Strategic and operational planning uses project management, process management, and practical tools and techniques to gather data, assess performance, plan the work, and work the plan. In fact, the creation of the *strategic plan* is almost anticlimactic. That is because the very nature of the process of planning goes far beyond the plan itself. The process of strategic planning, when done well, assesses performance and generates the information necessary to allow an organization to manage itself strategically. Not just once a year, but on an on-going, real-time basis. An overview of the strategic planning framework—approach, deployment, and results—is shown in figure 5.2.

---

[20] R. E. Miles and C. C. Snow, *Organization Strategy, Structure, and Process* (New York: McGraw-Hill, 1978).

Figure 5.2: Strategic Planning: Approach, Deployment, and Results

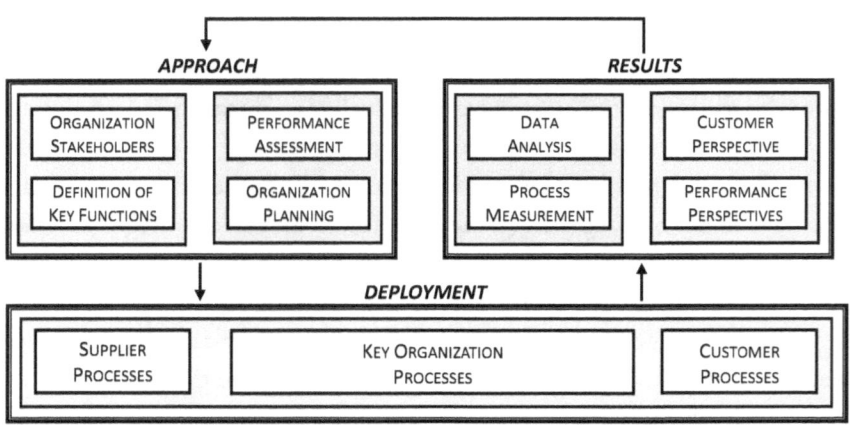

Depending on the approach taken, strategic planning consists of multiple phases that comprise multiple milestones. Each planning phase and milestone supports the strategic planning framework for the creation of a meaningful, usable strategic plan. At its foundation, the strategic planning process consists of integrating data from various sources, including process performance measures, customers, suppliers, research, and sponsorship. Once gathered, the data is analyzed, and a performance assessment of the organization's crucial processes is completed. Results from the performance assessment are used to drive the organization's strategic and operational plans. Periodically, progress reviews are fed back into the planning process along with updated performance assessment data. Strategic plans are adjusted, as necessary, and the process repeats itself.

Every leader, regardless of whether from the private, public, or nonprofit sector, or working in a large or small organization, must have a good understanding of strategic planning for two reasons:

> ➤ All leaders that have a desire to be successful need a process for managing strategic and operational change.
> ➤ Every leader in an organization is responsible for managing or executing one or more business outcomes.

Note: In our discussion of strategic planning, though "organization" is commonly applied in a macro sense—the whole organization—the reference (and, naturally, strategic and operational planning) can also be applied to a micro sense, that is, a division, unit, work group, etc.

Figure 5.3 (and, yes, it is daunting at first sight) represents a strategic planning framework comprised of five planning phases and twenty-four milestones that unpack the *approach*, *deployment*, and *results* presented in figure 5.2. The five phases (and the twenty-four milestones) are discussed individually and sequentially in this chapter. Though the milestones are listed sequentially, some may be accomplished simultaneously. Even so, it is a good practice to complete one milestone before beginning work on the next one. Subpar completion of a given step will more than likely result in wasted time and effort requiring going back and finishing the step properly. Finally, the skills, training, and knowledge required to develop and deploy strategic planning milestones must be present before work on each one can begin.

Typically, the initial strategic planning cycle takes between ten to twenty days and should be completed within four to six months. Thereafter, performance data is generated and assessed on an ongoing basis to help managers make important decisions regarding mission accomplishment.

Figure 5.3: Strategic Planning Framework

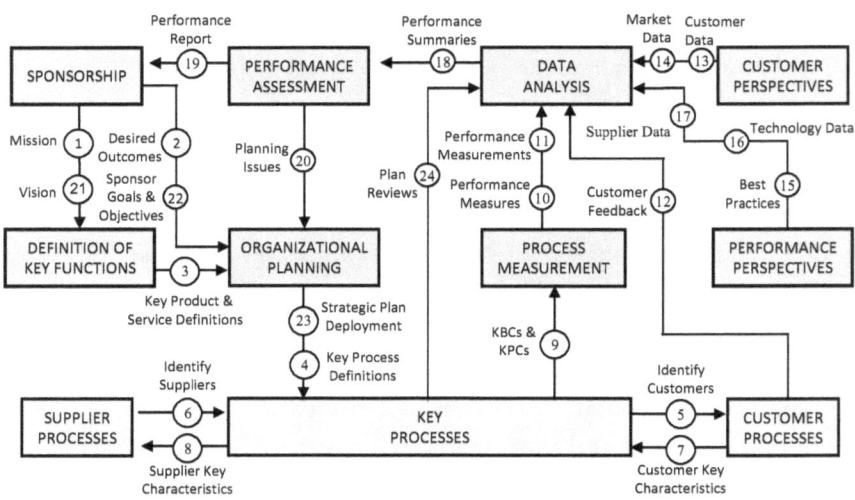

Understanding the strategic planning process can be daunting. The intention here is not to provide an "everything-you-need-to-know" explanation of how to do strategic planning properly; rather, it is to highlight the basic strategic planning process. Remember that successful strategic planning requires various people working together at every step. Brief descriptions of each phase and phase milestones are provided below.

PHASE 1: PURPOSE AND DIRECTION

This is the *getting to know the organization* and *getting started* phase. It begins with the organization's mission statement, which communicates the essence of an organization to stakeholders and customers, followed by a description of functions (and types of functions) engaged in by the organization, and finishes with a list of key strategic planning stakeholders—those who can significantly help or hinder the strategic planning process. While there is no magic formula for finding the wording that best expresses the organization's mission, it should succinctly state *who the organization is, what it does, for whom it does it*, and *why*. Phase 1 milestone descriptions follow:

➢ ①: The *mission statement* describes what the organization does and for whom.

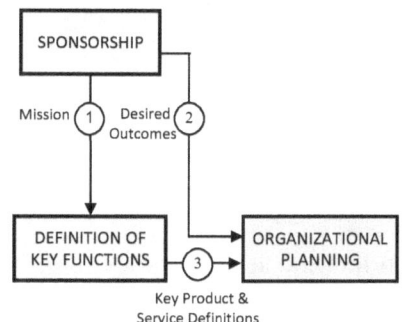

➢ ②: *Desired outcomes* communicate what stakeholders want from the organization in fulfillment of its mission.

➢ ③: *Identifies key organization programs, products, and services* that provide stakeholders with what they want—desired outcomes. The information gained from milestone #1 and milestone #2 are used to obtain an inventory of key product and service definitions—these definitions describe key items of value that an organization produces or provides.[21]

You may have noticed that creation or review of the vision statement, what the future should or can be, is not addressed in this phase. That is because it is not until after internal and external assessments are complete, and performance data is analyzed and interpreted, that the state of the organization is known (*where we are*); only then can we realistically address the organization's vision statement (*where we are going*). Even so, if the organization has a vision statement, it is appropriate to reference it here.

Finally, it is important to know and document core values and philosophies. These describe how an organization conducts itself in accomplishing its mission—they guide the way an organization does business. If not known, it is advisable to take time to identify and document them. Keep in mind that core values and philosophies not only reflect the values and philosophy of the executive team; they should also address the values and assumptions of the entire organization. Core values and philosophies should answer

---

[21] Products and services represent the outputs from the organization's processes that are produced and delivered to its customers. An organization typically produces from three to five primary products and services, which performs a function, which meets a need, which yields the value-added characteristic or attribute defined in the mission statement.

the following questions: What are the principles for which we want our organization to be known? What is important to consider if we are to accomplish our mission?

PHASE 2: INTERNAL ASSESSMENT

An internal assessment identifies performance strengths and weaknesses, and evaluates an organization's capacity to respond to challenges and opportunities. The internal assessment primarily examines key programs, products, and services that produce and provide desired outcomes. Phase 2 milestone descriptions follow:

> ➤ ④: Identifies and defines organization processes that produce, provide, or deliver key *programs, products,* and *services* that provide sponsors with what they want.
> ➤ ⑤ and ⑥: Identify *customers* and *suppliers* of key organization processes.
> ➤ ⑦ and ⑧: Define *customer requirements* and *supplier inputs* of key organization processes.
> ➤ ⑨: Defines *performance characteristics*—key business characteristics (KBCs) and key process characteristics (KPCs)—that the organization must do well in order to meet customer and mission requirements.
> ➤ ⑩ and ⑪: Establish quantitative *measures* and *measurements* to track achievement of desired outcomes, and process and organization performance.

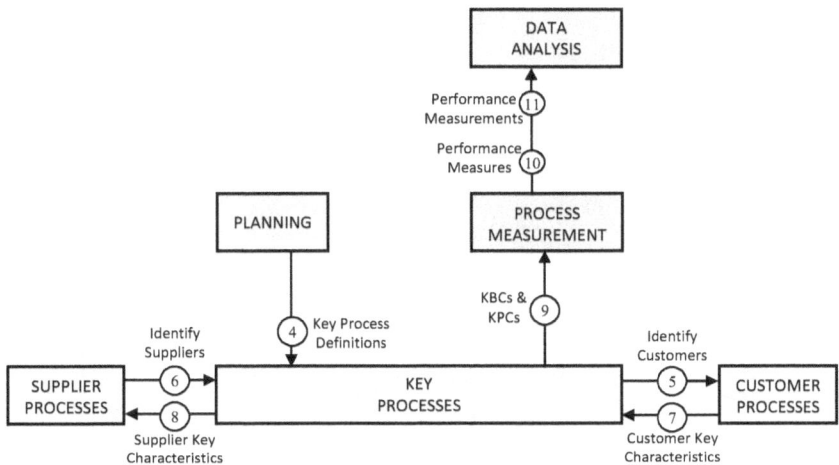

The internal assessment should answer the following questions (to list a few): What must the organization be good at? How do customers perceive the organization's programs, products, and services? Has the organization been stagnant or in decline? What has been accomplished and what remains to be accomplished? What has the organization done well, and how has it done it? Where has the organization been? Where is the organization now? What are the current programs or activities and what are their results? Are performance outcomes being met?

PHASE 3: EXTERNAL ASSESSMENT

An external assessment examines factors that affect the organization's ability to achieve desired results. Opportunities and threats are identified and studied. Critical planning issues facing the organization should surface in the external assessment. Phase 3 milestone descriptions follow:

> ⑫: Assesses *customer importance* and *satisfaction* with organization products and services (e.g., items of value).

➢ ⑬: Examines *how* and *why* customers use organization programs, products, and services, and what *customer needs* are met and unmet.

➢ ⑭: Gathers *market data* essential for evaluating organization strategies.

➢ ⑮: Identifies *best practices*—learn how and why things work the way they do.

➢ ⑯: Assesses the potential and limits of *technology*—considering how to enhance the use and application of technology.

➢ ⑰: Identifies potential *suppliers* of key process inputs.

Consider answering the following questions (to list a few) while completing this phase: How well have the needs of the customers been met? What elements of the current external environment are relevant to the organization? Which are most critical, most likely to facilitate or impede the organization? What are the current major issues or problems? Why are these of such importance? What current events or policy issues have captured the public's attention, and how do these affect the organization?

The knowledge gained in the external assessment—what is occurring or going to occur in an ever-changing environment—is intended to help the organization understand the environment in which it operates and to assess the impact of environmental forces (positive and negative) that can affect the organization's ability to achieve its mission.

PHASE 4: PERFORMANCE SUMMARIES AND REPORT

Access to meaningful, reliable data and having the ability to analyze and interpret data in context are essential for summarizing organizational performance. Performance summaries begin the ongoing process of analyzing the organization's internal and environmental data. It seeks to identify key factors likely to influence the organization's performance and the strategic planning process. By understanding and anticipating these factors, the organization is more likely to be successful. Phase 4 milestone descriptions follow:

> ⑱: *Performance summaries* analyze and interpret the organization's internal and environmental data in order to distinguish the important from the unimportant.
> ⑲: The *performance report* outlines where the organization is and what it wants to achieve.

Performance Report

Performance Summaries

| SPONSORSHIP | ⑲ | PERFORMANCE ASSESSMENT | ⑱ | DATA ANALYSIS |

Internal summaries represent how the organization is, or has been, performing: the *where we are*. External summaries involve sorting the mass of customer and performance perspectives data into a logical stream of useful information to reveal common themes and linkages. Monitoring, analysis, and reporting of performance summaries are used for organizational learning and growth, as well as to inform policy makers and other interested parties on progress toward achieving goals.

The performance report assesses and identifies gaps in current capabilities. Gaps in capabilities become the foundation for strategic and operational planning. If there are too many gaps to close all at once, then the report should prioritize gaps in service, separating the critical from the trivial. Preparing the report is similar to public speaking in the sense that one must know his or her audience—with whom is the organization intending to communicate? For the purposes of this report, it is the stakeholders and others as deemed necessary. So, write the performance report succinctly in terms meaningful to the key readers and users of the report.

PHASE 5: STRATEGIC PLAN CREATION AND DEVELOPMENT

Strategic direction is set by the organization's goals, objectives, and strategies; it is how the organization plans to achieve its vision and mission (see appendix 3 for an illustration of strategic plan alignment and deployment). It is at this point that an organization's knowledge and insights about past and present performance converge with desired future performance. Strategic plan creation and deployment determine how an organization will align its activities and its resources. Phase 5 milestone descriptions follow:

> ➤ ⑳: Identifies critical issues that are likely to, or will, affect strategic and operational planning resulting in clarifying needed modifications to programs, products, services, or delivery methods.
> ➤ ㉑: Creates a vision statement that describes where the organization wants to be.
> ➤ ㉒: Obtains sponsorship goals and objectives that focus the organization's planning efforts in a defined direction reflecting what the organization needs to achieve.
> ➤ ㉓ : Creates and deploys the plan; outlines how the organization will achieve what it wants.[22]
> ➤ ㉔ : Provides a check on the status and progress of strategic and operational plans so that deviations are analyzed and adjustments made.

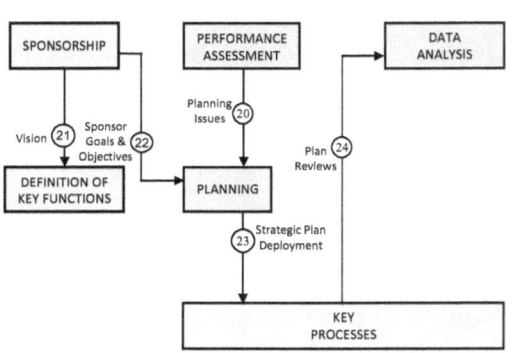

---

[22] Deployment basically means to assign ownership for implementation of the plan, and, naturally, to ensure the plan is resourced. Available resources, to include people's time, are among the most important considerations for achieving results. High ambitions are fine, but without sufficient time and budget, there is little hope for success. When MS #23 is complete, everyone in the organization should have responsibility for and understand the linkages of their part in the plan—whether it is strategic and/or operational plan implementation. So theoretically, everyone should be directly involved in the activities that contribute to the strategic direction of the organization.

Keep in mind that there is no magic formula by which a successful strategic plan is crafted. Key ingredients, though, are a combination of persistence, brilliance, discipline, foresight, experience, and, of course, luck. The planning horizon will vary depending on scope and scale, and whether the organization's external environment is stable or volatile. And, strategic planning never ends. Remember that planning entails real costs with respect to time and money. Staffing the strategic planning process is critical. Budgeting is also a very real part of implementing strategy. Not everyone can be involved in the process, and not everything can be fully funded.

As you can see, strategic plan creation and implementation is an essential management skill—a leadership nonnegotiable. Significant leadership and decision making in this area is needed (e.g., is the organization ready to undertake the strategic planning process, is the organization willing to commit the level of time and other resources necessary to plan strategically, are desired outcomes known or reasonably estimated, and who will participate in the strategic planning process?). Remember that strategic planning is not an individual effort; so think it through, set the vision, find your team, and lead the way.

CHAPTER 6

IMPLEMENTING CHANGE

As noted about strategic planning in chapter 5, the same is true for managing and implementing a change initiative: there is just too much to cover in one chapter. Moreover, too much information can complicate thinking, which may result in feeling overwhelmed, and even disillusioned. Instead, our intention here is to convey some essentials of managing change: what you should know that, when understood, will enhance the likelihood of being successful when it comes to implementing change. So, let's get started with an example that makes a critical point.

Six months of broad organizational effort on the part of others and myself produced an impressive understanding of corporate's *current state* matched with credible insights into its *future state*—one supported by detailed analysis and realistic plans for market growth, corporate positioning, and business development. It was time for the strategic planning team to report to the corporate executives. The majority of this briefing was spent describing the sequence of steps and quantifying resources needed to achieve corporate's strategic future. After the briefing, the CEO said, "Great job, everyone" and began to get up to leave the meeting.

"Wait." I interjected as I looked around the room. "Do we have approval to proceed [with implementation of the plan]?"

"Well," he replied, "I'll have to get back to you on that," and left the meeting.

What?! It was not just the strategic planning team that was onboard with this effort; it was one that had been generously supported by the CEO himself and staff alike. What was going on? The CEO's comment seemed strange and out of character. Something was wrong.

Two weeks later, I received an e-mail from the CEO confirming rumors that the corporation fell victim to a hostile takeover; under confidentiality, he was directed not to make any significant changes to corporate systems or processes until after an announcement of the "merger" and the new executive team was in place. After three months, the majority of senior officers had been replaced, had left, or were looking to leave; my team, too, was on the way out the door. Nothing in our plan saw this coming—the plan was dead.

Here is the point: it is *implementation* of the strategic plan that matters, not the *production* of it. Granted, a well-thought-out and developed strategic plan is essential for successful implementation, but the plan itself accomplishes little unless it is implemented. While the plan urges/outlines needed change, it is implementation/execution of the plan that creates change, and it is the presence of change that drives improvement/progress. In other words, we *plan* so we can meaningfully implement; we *implement* so we can purposefully change; and we *change* so we can *improve*—get better at what we do, do what we do differently, or learn to do something altogether different.

We plan to implement → We implement to change → We change to improve

While change does not always equal improvement, improvement most always results from change. Einstein's definition of insanity seems appropriate here: "Doing the same thing over and over and expecting a different result." Want a different result, then something must change. Change, whether happening to us or driven by us, is a fact of life. We must be resilient with the former and deliberate with the latter.

Furthermore, we must realize, understand, and accept that we do not live in a perfect world, but rather, we live in the real world, one without full knowledge of *what is* and foresight of *what is to come*. I say this because too many executives expect perfect plans when they do not exist. As a consequence of this, some critical *understandings* of strategic planning and implementation should be kept in mind:

> ➤ We must *understand* that something, somewhere, will surface that disrupts or influences planning, implementation, or both that will cause planning, implementation, or both to change.
> ➤ We must *understand* that even the best planners cannot account for everything—something, somewhere, will get missed, unaccounted for, under/overestimated, etc., that will cause planning, implementation, or both to change.

Effects of these understandings, both good and bad, are inevitable; so changes—due to external and internal forces—to plans and their implementation are business-as-usual. For example, *external forces* (e.g., an economic correction, a competitor exiting a market, repeated customer complaints about a service) may cause changes to the plan and/or implementation in order to pursue opportunities or to avoid emerging threats. Or, perhaps, plan and/or implementation changes are driven by *internal forces* (e.g., a new product innovation from research and development, unexpected turnover, or newly articulated performance goals) that reveal dissatisfaction with what is or dreams of what could be.

When done properly, strategic planning will assess not only what has previously changed—intentionally or unintentionally—but what needs to change. Naturally, bringing a new or revised plan to life may require changes to the organization's structure, staffing, skill sets, culture, processes, reward systems, and so on. Though the list of things that *could* change is not exhaustive, thinking about what will need to change and the efforts necessary to implement change can be exhausting.

STRATEGIC MANAGEMENT AND CHANGE MANAGEMENT

The processes of strategic management and change management are inseparable. Through a well-executed strategic planning process, leaders reveal, and then communicate, why an organization should change. Communicating the "why" in a pervasive way requires a messenger with personal character and leadership talent. It also requires substantive and credible information (data), as the goal is to build and sustain commitment toward the change. Once the reasons—the *why*—for change are known and conveyed, attention shifts to *where* the change is needed, *what* needs to change, *who* will need to change, and by *when* the change should be completed. We can only discuss the *how* when we have clarity as to the *why* and then the *where*, *what*, *who*, and *when*.

A statistic commonly cited is that 70 to 80 percent of change efforts fail.[23] While personal experiences (and research) may vary regarding the validity of this statistic, I'm sure we can all agree that planned change rarely results in complete fulfillment of desired outcomes—fulfillment to some degree, sure, but complete fulfillment is a rare thing indeed. Frankly, implementing organizational change is hard. As noted about leadership, there is no perfect model, recipe, or checklist that, if followed, guarantees success. Why? Because both strategic management and change management, and the environments in which they exist, are imperfect. Furthermore, within those environments, organizational dynamics, competition for scarce resources, corporate politics, and so much more create competing plans and agendas, ones that do not always agree with or support your plan for change. Like snowflakes, each change is unique. Change initiatives are launched with little certainty—no guarantees—as to how they will unfold and ultimately end. From the outset, leaders must create commitment to the desired change as well as sustain that commitment over time. Many change efforts stall or are derailed as people lose interest or become preoccupied with other things. Finally, time itself works against efforts to effect change. As time passes, new external and internal forces appear that can render a given change less important or even eliminate the need for the planned change in the first place.

From the outset, leaders should seriously consider the *magnitude* of change being planned. Magnitude focuses attention on the size (scale and scope) of an intended change initiative (see figure 6.1). For example, is change isolated to the individual employee-level (e.g., a job rotation program), corporate-level (e.g., a succession plan), or somewhere in between?

---

[23] M. Hughes, "Do 70 percent of all organizational change efforts really fail?" *Journal of Change Management,* 2011.

Figure 6.1: Organization Scale and Scope

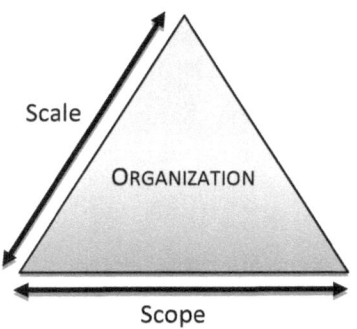

In the case of Therese, she was tasked with reenergizing an underperforming region in the organization. The changes she considered included: reorganization of positions, staff changes (including adding or eliminating jobs) and, ultimately, targeted efforts at altering the region's culture. Large-scale, big-change projects typically happen when entire divisions, regions, or an organization is targeted (e.g., an internal reorganization of divisions or an acquisition of, or merger with, another company). As the magnitude of change increases, so does the complexity of the change initiative as well as the time necessary to plan and, then, execute the change. Large-scale—heavy-lifting—change projects invariably involve multiple "smaller" change initiatives that need to be properly paced and sequenced together.

It is the presence of magnitude and complexity that promotes appreciation for and use of change models to enhance our understanding of the change process. In that regard, the change literature is rife with three-stage change models. These models are helpful—to a point—as they can help one better understand the importance of time as it relates to the flow of change. The most famous three-stage model comes from Kurt Lewin.[24] Lewin's model outlines how an organization has to *unfreeze* the status quo (e.g., address directly the inertia that prevents one from making the change) before one implements the change (characterized by *moving*). Once implemented, the change should then be *frozen* (e.g., provided with the necessary time

---

[24] S. Cummings, T. Bridgman, and K. G. Brown. "Unfreezing change as three steps: Rethinking Kurt Lewin's legacy for change management," *Human Relations*, 2015.

and resources to take hold). Comparable three-stage models are provided in table 6.1. Again, a word of caution: these change models, because they make intuitive sense, and do serve a purpose, which is to help initially frame the change process. They provide little help in actually leading the change.

Table 6.1: Three-Stage Change Models[25]

	THE CHANGE PROCESS STAGES		
Lewin (1947)	Unfreezing	Moving	Refreezing
Beckhard & Harris (1977)	Present state	Transition state	Future state
Nadler & Tushman (1989)	Energizing	Envisioning	Enabling
Bridges (2003)	Ending, letting go	Neutral zone	New beginning
Warrick (2005)	Preparing for change	Implementing change	Sustaining change

The remainder of the chapter focuses on three issues pertinent to the leadership nonnegotiables. Successful change begins with leaders who possess personal character, leadership talent, and management skill. Armed with character, talent, and skill, leaders are then positioned to (1) simultaneously pursue organization stability and flexibility, (2) attend to change readiness and resistance, and (3) effectively (and consistently) listen and communicate about a given change initiative.

We make no promises that change is easy. It is true that change can turn ugly, especially if the benefits have been overestimated and the costs underestimated. However, as noted by Jeffrey Pfeffer and Bob Sutton, despite the costs, risks, and horror stories associated with change, refusing to change is not the answer either. [26] The only thing more dangerous than conducting change is never doing it at all.

---

[25] Adapted from "Developing organization change champions," D. D. Warrick, *OD Practitioner*, 2009.

[26] J. Pfeffer and R. I. Sutton, *Hard Facts, Dangerous Half-truths, and Total Nonsense: Profiting from Evidence-based Management* (Cambridge, MA: Harvard University Press, 2006).

The "old school" notion that to bring about change one needed to build urgency because of some threat is just that: *old*. Consider this: the best time to change may be when things are going well; that is, to change *before* one needs to change. In such instances, there is urgency, but the urgency is about sustaining something *positive*.

There are no fail-safe answers to ensure your success at leading change. Although you might question whether you are the person to lead the change, that there may be somebody better, or even whether you should bother in the first place, it is important to remember that change cannot be left to chance. Also remember you are not alone. Successful change requires engaged individuals—individuals with personal character, leadership talent, and management skills—at all levels over time.

STABILITY AND FLEXIBILITY

Organizations exist to produce—be it a product, service, or information. Because organizations cannot ignore the daily demands of being just that, a business, leaders cannot underestimate the importance that hierarchy and requisite managerial processes play in the support and success of that business. Specifically, organizations, to operate efficiently and effectively, require *stability* built around policies and standard operating practices. This stability comes from the formal organization structure and the designation of responsibility for a given job at a given level. However, the formal organization is not adept at *flexibility*. What the formal organization does not do well is identify the most important hazards and opportunities early enough, formulate creative strategic initiatives nimbly enough, and implement them fast enough.[27] In other words, the formal organization commonly fails to make needed, timely change (especially when *it* is what must be changed).

---

[27] J. P. Kotter, "Accelerate! How the most innovative companies capitalize on today's rapid-fire strategic changes—and still make their numbers," *Harvard Business Review,* November 2012.

What is a change leader to do? A common theme associated with organizational change and success is ambidexterity.[28] An organization (and, thus, a change leader) must be able to both exploit *what it currently does well* while simultaneously exploring *what it could do better*.[29] Again, it is the formal organization that should be more adept—more efficient and more effective—at exploiting these lanes of opportunity and growth. As for exploration, the solution is a second "operating" system (or informal organization) devoted to exploration, and to the development and implementation of strategy.[30] The informal organization represents an agile, network-like structure where the talents of diverse employees are brought together in teams.

These teams draw individuals from different units and different hierarchical levels from across the organization—freed from the formal organizational structure—to continually assess the organization and its relationship to its environment. By operating outside the rigid hierarchy, these teams are expected to react to emerging change as well as implement planned change with greater agility, speed, and creativity than the formal organization. Like the relationship between leadership and management, the informal organization complements—not overburdens—the traditional hierarchy. Working together, there is a constant flow of information and activity between them. Both systems *learn* with and from the other.

So to adapt to external and internal forces, organizations (like individuals, teams, and units) must be simultaneously stable and flexible. This is the very challenge Therese faced when she became the director of the new region. Therese had to keep the region focused on its day-to-day job (the present) while also developing a new strategy and implementing the changes needed to turn the strategy from a paper document into reality (the future). As the regional director, Therese was responsible for the formal organization and for creating the informal organization.

---

[28] C. A. O'Reilly III and M. L. Tushman, "Organizational ambidexterity: Past, present, and future," *Academy of Management Perspectives*, 2013.

[29] J. March, "Exploration and exploitation in organizational learning," *Organization Science*, 1991.

[30] Kotter, "Accelerate!"

The challenges faced by anyone in Therese's shoes are best represented by a quote from F. Scott Fitzgerald: "The test of a first-rate intelligence is the ability to hold two opposed ideas in the mind at the same time, and still retain the ability to function. One should, for example, be able to see that things are hopeless and yet be determined to make them otherwise." How does Therese do this? How does she navigate two systems? We refer back to chapter 4 and the discussion on staffing. To succeed, and for her own well-being, Therese must: (1) ensure the right people are placed in key jobs in the *formal* organization, and (2) bring together the best people as she shapes the *informal* organization. She must also contemplate the *magnitude* of intended changes, revising her perceptions and, thus, plans on a daily basis. This allows her to keep abreast of where the change should be occurring, and whether the *pacing* and *sequencing* of change efforts are unfolding in a timely manner. While Therese is able to make changes to the region's policies and structure relatively quickly, making some key personnel changes may take longer. Even more challenging is Therese's determination to influence the region's culture; that will likely involve multiple interventions over an extended period of time.

Remember that as the regional director, Therese has a lot going on—both within the region (formal and informal structures and networks) and beyond the region (other regions, corporate headquarters, and stakeholders). Implementing changes, whatever they may be, will likely require broad-based region- and corporate-wide buy-in and support. Additionally, there will be costs (tangible and intangible) associated with her efforts. For the tangibles, she will have to prepare budgets, develop measures, and communicate progress (and the value added/return-on-investment) of the planned changes. For the intangibles, she will have to keep her finger on the pulse of region and corporate morale and motivation in order to maintain support for and sustain her change efforts. At times she will need to be simultaneously work-focused and people-focused. While intent to listen and collaborate, Therese will also need to be decisive when decisions are needed. Progress toward realizing change requires working with others while ensuring the necessary work is completed.

READINESS AND RESISTANCE

Oftentimes, significant changes are announced through an organization-wide e-mail or a town hall meeting of employees. Considering your experience, what has been your initial reaction to such announcements? Was it excitement? Bewilderment—not needed? Dread—won't work? An inaudible "Oh brother, here we go again?" Or, perhaps a blank stare, or outright resistance. Beyond the initial reaction, have you ever wondered why you react as you do to such announcements?

Jeffrey and Laurie Ford suggest that initial plans for change can be met with complacency, resignation, and cynicism (see table 6.2).[31] *Complacency* reflects a person's (or group's) perception that nothing new or different is needed. Given this perception, a person may question the need to change the status quo even while acknowledging things may not be perfect. For the change leader, the anecdote for complacency is providing convincing evidence of the need for change as well as specifics as to why change now (not later), and translating that evidence and specifics into credible explanations/reasons for implementing change.

Table 6.2: Reactions to Change

REACTION	CHANGE BELIEF	BLAME FOR FAILURE
Complacency	Change not needed	-
Resignation	Change won't work	Self
Cynicism	Change won't work	Others

Resignation and *cynicism* may be more gradual, subtle, and harmful than complacency in that both reflect a belief that any planned change just won't work. What distinguishes resignation from cynicism is where blame for failure is placed. When resigned, individuals blame their own lack of ability to bring about change. Examples of resignation statements include: "We have no idea what our customers want" or "We discuss what needs to change, and we make a lot of plans, but it stops there." Cynicism places

---

[31] J. D. Ford and L. W. Ford, "Stop blaming resistance to change and start using it," *Organization Dynamics*, 2010.

the blame on others who frustrate and disappoint attempts at change. Here organizational members state: "Headquarters wants us to improve, but they always sabotage our best efforts with impossible demands and lack of resources." Clearly, resignation and cynicism reflect trust issues: trust among us and with others. The challenge for those leading change is to alter existing perceptions of self and others; namely, to convince individuals to have trust in their own knowledge, skills, and abilities to influence and effect change themselves as well as to build trust in others—usually through relationship/team building—to influence and effect change together. To accomplish this, trust in the leaders—leaders with the credibility and reputation—is needed to overcome beliefs that the change is not needed and/or the change won't work.

All three—complacency, resignation, and cynicism—can be evident simultaneously across organizational members. Statements by leaders that things will be different this time are not enough to combat resignation and cynicism. When faced with either, change leaders must first build trust, and this takes time, patience, and discipline.

Adding to the challenges faced by leaders that a change is "not needed" or "won't work" is the perception that the organization is always changing. In some organizations, one change initiative is never fully completed before one or more other changes are simultaneously launched. When this occurs repeatedly, employees are susceptible to "change fatigue." While not complacent or resigned, they do want a break from all the change. The seemingly never-ending cycle of change is both cognitively and emotionally taxing.

In an extreme case where an organization needs to change or find itself out of business, people have no other choice but to be open to and grudgingly ready for the changes to come. In such a case, acceptance for the need to change and motivation are generally high—it's do or die, figuratively speaking; there is no other choice. Those in the earlier story of the hostile takeover/merger found themselves in a similar circumstance; go with the flow (change) or leave. In less extreme cases—those where associated risks and consequences are less severe—leaders cannot take others' acceptance and motivation for a change effort for granted. Given the real threats of complacency, resignation, cynicism, and change fatigue, leaders should first evaluate an organization's readiness for change before launching a change initiative. Given the current state of organizational *readiness*, perhaps the answer to change is not no, just not now, not yet.

So what do we mean by readiness? At the *individual level*, an individual's readiness for change is reflected by the extent to which he or she is both cognitively and emotionally inclined to accept, embrace, and adopt a particular plan to purposefully alter the status quo.[32] Note the words *accept*, *embrace*, and *adopt*. These three words *together* equate to commitment. Committed employees are motivated to implement the change and see it succeed—at least initially. The question remains, however, whether initial commitment can be sustained. At a work group or *organizational level*, change readiness is influenced by the shared beliefs that the change is needed, the group or organization has the capability to successfully undertake the change, and the change will have positive outcomes for the individuals, the work group, and the organization.[33]

The situation Therese faced when taking over as the new regional director provides us an excellent example. Changes were necessary, otherwise she would not have been asked to take on that responsibility. From the moment her appointment was announced, she was on the clock with respect to assessing individuals' and the region's readiness for change—recall Therese's phone calls to key stakeholders, staff, union members, and outgoing director even before she arrived at the region in order to get their perspectives. The calls were not only done to assess readiness but to build a base of trust—get buy-in—to support the inevitable changes yet to come. Building both readiness and trust needed to happen as quickly as the situation would allow. The most untenable situation for a leader is when there is a pervasive belief that change is not necessary and when there

---

[32] D. R. Holt, A. A. Armenakis, H. S. Field, and S. G. Harris, "Readings for organizational change: The systematic development of a scale," *Journal of Applied Behavioral Science,* 2007.

[33] A. E. Rafferty, N. L. Jimmieson, and A. A. Armenakis, "Change readiness: A multilevel review," *Journal of Management,* 2013.

is high mistrust of those charged with bringing about change—Therese's situation to a tee.

Though the region's employees knew changes, significant changes, were coming, there was pent-up opposition to change even before it was known where, what, or who might change. Recall Therese's description of the "blame game" within the region. People knew the region had problems but believed the causes of performance problems were the fault of others, not themselves. The "blame game" is particularly intractable because people are looking to others to change: "It is *their* fault. *They* are the reason we face these problems. *They* need to take the first step." By focusing on "why us?" such individuals have forgotten that the only thing they have control over is their own beliefs and behavior.

As for mistrust, well, her every move and decision was being watched and critiqued. Moreover, mistrust did not reside with Therese alone; it was prevalent throughout the region. Thus, her initial actions and the perceptions they created had huge influences/consequences for her and the region as a whole. If she wanted the cooperation of the region's employees, they had to trust her, and she had to trust they would commit to the planned change.

Change leaders like Therese seek to build and sustain momentum toward realizing the desired change outcomes. They address *why* this is the right time to change. They continually convey a compelling argument, delivered in multiple and inspiring ways, for the change. They reinforce what needs to change while also outlining what won't change. They emphasize the benefits associated with the change are more than the costs associated with not changing. By leveraging their personal character, focusing on individual and group needs, and providing credible information, what they hope to witness, as they speak to or meet with employees, are heads nodding in affirmation. They hope to hear talk of how the change plan makes sense to those who will be implementing and experiencing the change. When people sense greater trust than mistrust, greater openness than reticence, and greater readiness than resistance to change, then there is true momentum toward realizing change. When this happens the change becomes less dependent on a given change leader and more the result of collective action.

A word of caution: creating readiness for change does not eliminate potential resistance to the planned change or the various efforts to bring about change; even stakeholders may resist change. Just because an individual, unit, or organization needs to change—and may be ready to change— there are no guarantees there will be no resistance to it. Several sources of resistance have already been noted: (1) the costs of the change are more than the benefits, (2) it is the wrong time to change, (3) the reasons for the change have been poorly communicated, and (4) the change initiative has been poorly planned and/or implemented. Organizational and personal sources of resistance are listed in table 6.3.

Table 6.3: Sources of Resistance

Organizational	• Lack of trust in management (poor leadership)
	• Poor communication
	• Lack of training
	• Lack of support (especially from top management), including inadequate resources
	• Past failures of change
	• Organizational politics, power, and other conflicts
	• Organizational culture
Personal	• Fear of change (and/or) love the current routine
	• Fear of the unknown
	• Fear of failure
	• Self-interest
	• Lack of rewards or motivation
	• Loss of job, control, or comfort
	• Increased workload

Resistance can manifest itself at any point during the change process, and when it does, it needs to be addressed because its presence can divert attention and consume precious energy. While organizational sources of resistance expose problems with *how the change is getting accomplished*, personal sources of resistance expose the concerns of individuals with respect to *what will happen or is happening to them.*

For many years, resistance was considered to be a negative consequence of change. The presumption was that change leaders, like Therese, were doing right by the organization while those expected to change were *irrational* and stuck in their ways; and while leaders planned and encouraged change, those expected to change would throw up obstacles and barriers to change. Thus, resistance threatened most every change effort. Resistance was something that needed to be eliminated as soon as possible.

However, Jeffrey and Laurie Ford have questioned this resistance-as-a-negative view.[34] Instead, *resistance paradoxically may be a critical factor in the success of change efforts.* Unlike the threats posed by complacency, resignation, and/or cynicism, they suggest resistance should be viewed as an asset. Regardless of your point-of-view, it is well understood (from research and past experiences) that outright attempts to squash resistance often only intensifies it as well as fosters complacency, resignation, or cynicism. Like Therese when she faced resistance on multiple fronts, it is important to understand opposing perspectives, communicate openly, and invite people to participate in the change process.

With respect to the readiness-resistance relationship, change leaders need to develop readiness, but they must also surface resistance, getting it out into the open so it can be addressed and dealt with. Addressing resistance is linked to keeping individuals and the organization change ready. Openly working with resistance helps to improve readiness, and improved readiness helps to forestall further resistance. Paramount to ensuring readiness is how leaders listen and communicate.

LISTENING AND COMMUNICATING

It has been said that at least 51 percent of communicating is listening. If there is one lesson from our discussion of resistance it is this: listening to

---

[34] Ford and Ford, "Stop blaming resistance."

and understanding others' reactions to a proposed change is imperative. A commitment to and demonstration of active listening engenders trusting relationships. That being said, do not mistake a person's less than enthusiastic reaction to change as resistance to change; likewise, disagreement is not resistance; blatant attempts to stop change is resistance. In other words, reactions and disagreements should not be equated with resistance or obstruction of change initiatives.

In addition, change leaders must attentively listen to not only what *is* said, but what *is not* being said. Silence, too, communicates,[35] but what it communicates is often left to others' interpretations. For example, silence may be interpreted as agreement, the withholding of or lack of information, dissent, or belief that saying anything would be futile or even detrimental to one's career. For someone to speak up, there must be belief that what *is* said will matter, and that their concerns will be listened to and understood. Otherwise, employees would rather suffer in silence, believing that by doing so, they can outlast those pushing the change and, thus, the change itself.

Without knowing the new region fully, Therese had to assume her arrival would be met, to some degree, with silence. Recall she even described the region's climate as one of reservation. To be successful, she had to get people to believe that she was truly interested in hearing what they had to say, and that what they said would not be ignored or used against them. The work by Jeffrey and Laurie Ford is instructive here.[36] They argue that successful change depends on the interplay of four equally important conversation types: initiating conversations, understanding conversations, performance conversations, and closure conversations.

> ➤ *Initiating conversations* are about starting the change (and any associated interventions). The focus is on the *why*.

---

[35] C. C. Pinder and K. P. Harlos, "Employee silence: Quiescence and acquiescence as responses to perceived injustice," *Research in Personnel and Human Resources Management*, 2011.
[36] For more information, see J. D. Ford and L.W. Ford, *The four conversations: Daily communication that gets results* (San Francisco: Berrett-Koehler, 2009).

➢ *Understanding conversations* are about developing a common language among participants. By doing so, a shared context is created in which people learn how to talk to each other about the changes. This shared context should translate into greater knowledge of what change success will look like, and the level of participation and support needed to make this success a reality.

➢ *Performance conversations* are about producing the intended results. These conversations address the *what, who, when, where,* and *how* questions. They set expectations about accountability and the timeline for achieving goals.

➢ *Closure conversations* are about completing the change. If we consider the three-stage change models introduced earlier in this chapter, closure is essential for change. This is when equilibrium (stability) is restored. It is through these conversations that leaders can ensure individual and organizational readiness for the next change. Finally, closure conversations acknowledge that there are now new possibilities and new futures that did not exist prior to the most recent change efforts.

Therese's change efforts began with initiating and understanding conversations. Such conversations provide the detail and context for framing, executing, and achieving desired change outcomes. It is important to note that change, and the conversations themselves, do not move linearly through the four conversations. There is no set pattern or frequency. As any change effort unfolds, change interventions are being implemented and tracked, and there is the need to clarify what is happening, remind people why it is happening, etc. Sometimes, unforeseen events require initiating other smaller changes that support the desired change outcome.

Keeping the four conversations in mind is important when the change effort stalls. When this occurs, leaders should look to the conversations occurring about the change. Instead of the usual culprit—resistance—it is possible one or two types of conversations are dominating the change discussions at the expense of the other types. How often have you heard the comment: "All we seem to do is talk about the change and what should be done, but nothing ever happens"? Does that statement sound familiar?

If so, could it be that the majority of the change conversations fall into the initiating and/or understanding categories? Are conversations about actually executing the change rare?

Change leaders should track, at least to some extent, the range of conversations regarding change. Luckily, the Fords have outlined a process where change leaders can keep a log of their conversations for one to two weeks.[37] From this log, change leaders are able to check the frequency of the four conversation types. And, if there is an imbalance among the four conversation types, they can change what is being said (or not said) by themselves and others—especially in meetings—to jumpstart the change efforts. This same imbalance can occur with the six leadership styles first discussed in chapter 3, consequently affecting the planned change and its ultimate success. When change leaders become too work-focused or commanding/decisive when implementing the change, they ignore the coaching/mentoring or listening/collaboration needed to keep people committed to the desired change. On the other hand, overemphasis on visioning/dreaming with little movement toward implementing the change can result in people eventually tuning out. Whether one considers the four conversations or the six leadership styles, maintaining *balance* among them is key.

In closing this chapter, let's revisit Therese one more time. She was named as the region's new director to bring about change to an underperforming region. Her new assignment required her to seek stability and flexibility simultaneously, to address both change readiness and resistance, and to communicate and listen. Under the best of circumstances, she was taking over a region desperately needing change, yet unenthusiastic for it. Regardless, she knew there was no perfect road map to follow, one that would provide all the answers to launching and executing change. All she could do was build relationships with people who were also committed to creating a better future. And continuing to listen and learn was critical.

---

[37] J. D. Ford and L. W. Ford, "Conversational profiles: A tool for altering the conversational patterns of change managers," *Journal of Applied Behavioral Science,* 2008.

CHAPTER 7

LEADERSHIP NONNEGOTIABLES REVISITED

Let's recall the story of Therese from chapter 1. Her directive from senior executives was to improve performance, morale, and customer satisfaction at the troubled region. Though Therese had a proven record of performance and a solid reputation as a leader, past success did not ensure her future success. Even so, senior executives were banking on it. Though the story of Therese could have ended in various ways, after a year on the job, performance, morale, and customer satisfaction steadily improved; she earned personal credibility and restored position credibility, and the majority of region staff were finally working together. In reading this book, how she was able to accomplish this should not be all that surprising.

Recall, too, that the region was bleeding precious energy, resources, and talent. And that senior executives were not the only ones vested in the prospects for change; region staff also wanted relief from the despair of repetitive performance problems. No one was happy. Though everyone knew something had to change, there was no agreement on what needed to change and how best to change it.

Beyond leadership (people) needs, Therese knew she had to attend to the underlying system of management (things) that supports performance. Before she even arrived at the new region, her conversations with key staff had exposed serious concerns regarding customer dissatisfaction, low employee morale, and personnel conflicts. These concerns, she surmised, were indications of a much bigger problem related to production and service delivery, and that they were symptoms of a malfunctioning system, not dysfunctional people. Though confident in a course of action, Therese thought if she acted alone, most of the staff would think it was a repeat of past directors' behaviors, and, accordingly, staff would fail to support whatever change she decided. So, moving forward, decision making had to be a collaborative effort—buy-in was essential.

Therese also realized that whatever changes were implemented would have ramifications and affect a lot of people. Keeping the region functioning while supporting needed changes was a top priority. Figuratively, Therese had to change a tire on a moving car. This she could not accomplish alone. So she created a *guidance team*—a small team of five people composed of key union, management, and staff—separate from the normal hierarchy to explore the region's challenges and opportunities. This team took the long view, looking beyond immediate symptoms to uncover and fix underlying problems. This team was Therese's way of bringing together, and valuing, differing and distinctive voices. Building consensus and commitment through dialogue and action was of great importance.

Therese strongly believed that without the appearance and substance of this guidance team, there would be no driving or supporting force to implement needed change. Thus, the team was charged with developing the strategies for improving regional performance, customer satisfaction, and employee morale. Ultimately, recommendations for change and allocation of resources would come from the guidance team—though it did not operate in isolation. Therese guided, approved, and supported their efforts. She, especially, played a pivotal role in keeping the guidance team and the region's management team talking to each other and in keeping them focused on one mission, one purpose—improving region performance. Both teams relied on each other and shared the same staffing, budgeting, and production data with which to fulfill their respective functions.

Once the guidance team got up and running, it canvassed the regional staff, managers, stakeholders, and representative customers and suppliers for a list of business functions, areas, concerns, etc., that needed improvement.

From that list, priorities were identified, and, ultimately, the team identified six key projects. Each of these projects identified problem areas that had direct mission impact, were supported by performance data, were areas that internal and external stakeholders complained about, and were manageable in size and complexity. Identifying and scoping the six projects took four weeks.

Understanding that introducing six projects simultaneously would overwhelm the region and compete for everyone's attention, the team turned its attention to prioritizing and pacing the six projects. Three projects, with Therese's backing, were deemed to be needed now, and they would be introduced first. As implementation unfolded, Therese monitored the improvements while focusing on day-to-day performance (which was showing signs of improvement). Along the way, she heralded teamwork, recognized performance, and welcomed feedback. By the time the guidance team had completed its initial work on the three projects, Therese was hearing positive talk about the changes and seeing tangible improvements in production and service delivery. Though the guidance team (and Therese) had been working under an initial shadow of caution, given the recent results, upcoming changes were more readily accepted—resistance to change had mostly faded.

Naturally, as Therese continued to lead, the perceptions of her by superiors, peers, subordinates, customers, and stakeholders evolved. One of the many lessons to learn from Therese was her ever-present focus on the mission (purpose) and her high regard for those (people) performing the mission. Her actions and behaviors translated into her being seen by others as capable, credible, and competent. A leader is always "on stage." Moreover, Therese demonstrated four overarching orientations necessary for effective leadership. Those orientations are: task, relations, change, and external.[38] The four orientations are defined in table 1.

---

[38] G. Yukl, "Effective leadership behavior: What we know and what questions need more attention," *Academy of Management Perspectives*, 2012.

Table 1: Leadership Orientations and Styles

LEADERSHIP ORIENTATIONS	RELEVANT LEADERSHIP STYLES
Task-oriented—ability to plan and clarify, monitor operations, problem solve	Work focused Commanding-decisive Coach-mentor
Relations-oriented—adept at supporting, developing, recognizing, and empowering others	People-focused Coach-mentor Listener-collaborator
Change-oriented—ability to advocate and envision change, encourage innovation	Coach-mentor Listener-collaborator Visionary-dreamer
External-oriented—ability to network and represent outside the organization, monitor the external environment	Listener-collaborator Visionary-dreamer

Like the leadership nonnegotiables and the leadership styles (discussed in chapter 3), the orientations are not independent of each other. Instead, they are interdependent. While the use of such terms as "orientation", "style", and "nonnegotiable" may appear redundant or confusing, none of the three alone provides a complete picture of leadership. Together, however, they do. Further, it is the presence of the three nonnegotiables and their relationship to the orientations and styles that unite to inspire and achieve leadership outcomes. Therese's story was woven throughout this book because she exhibited personal character, leadership talent, and management skill. Her continuing success is also rooted in how she navigated being simultaneously task-oriented, relations-oriented, change-oriented, and external-oriented. Therese could not come in and *manage* the region out of its current performance funk. She had to lead by applying—depending on what the situation dictated at the time—the six leadership styles. And, as has been repeated in this book, she could not do it alone. She had to create an environment where others could participate—and lead—as well. A final important piece of information from Therese's story is her willingness, when the situation called for it, to step back and be led by others.

We expect leaders to produce results, and, invariably, we look for that "heroic" individual who can focus our attention and efforts to accomplish a desired outcome. However, such outcomes are rarely the result of one individual. Therese knew this. Throughout this book, we have spoken directly to you, the reader, that leadership is often distributed—shared among and accompanied by the talents of others. For leadership to work, the three nonnegotiables must be understood and present. More importantly, those who have clarity with respect to their own personal character, leadership talent, and management skills can better manage it in themselves as well as recognize it in others. Consequently, leaders mutually reinforce the efforts of other leaders.

Well, this concludes *Leadership Nonnegotiables*. I will close with the overriding theme repeated throughout the book: while there is *no substitute for personal character* (as it must always be present), elements of *leadership talent* and *management skill* can be shared or distributed among individuals. Though trite, it takes a village of individuals—leaders and managers, as well as leaders who can manage, and managers who can lead—to build, sustain, and change an organization. As a result, leaders and followers must recognize and accept that the majority of leadership outcomes require teamwork—everyone contributing toward a shared goal or purpose.

APPENDIX 1

LEADERSHIP ASSESSMENT— ABBREVIATED

Based on the book *Competent Leadership: Presenting the Knowledge to Lead, along with the Practical Lessons and Experience to Do It Well.*

Instructions: Start each sentence with "I," then circle the response that best describes what you would do. If assessing someone else, adjust language as needed.	most always	often	some times	rarely	almost never
1. ... nurture, develop, and motivate others.	5	4	3	2	1
2. ... win others' support for my ideas.	5	4	3	2	1
3. ... am confident and decisive in a crisis.	5	4	3	2	1
4. ... persist in seeking understanding despite difficulties.	5	4	3	2	1
5. ... promote harmony, unity, and build constructive relationships.	5	4	3	2	1
6. ... demonstrate high standards and a strong drive for achievement.	5	4	3	2	1
7. ... consider the person's knowledge, skills, abilities, and confidence to do a task.	5	4	3	2	1
8. ... communicate a sense of purpose and focus for tasks.	5	4	3	2	1

9. ... provide structure, rigid controls, and issue instructions without asking for input.	5	4	3	2	1
10. ... am considered to be a superb listener, collaborator, and influencer.	5	4	3	2	1
11. ... recognize the emotional needs of others.	5	4	3	2	1
12. ... am performance driven and maintain high levels of production.	5	4	3	2	1
13. ... provide challenging assignments to develop capabilities and confidence.	5	4	3	2	1
14. ... can inspire and rally others to contribute to your vision.	5	4	3	2	1
15. ... am sought out in a crisis.	5	4	3	2	1
16. ... respond to comments (good and bad) in a way that reflects understanding.	5	4	3	2	1
17. ... seek to resolve conflict and misunderstandings.	5	4	3	2	1
18. ... work with vigor, effectiveness, and determination over a sustained period.	5	4	3	2	1

Assessment Scoring and Feedback

Topic	Questions	Total
Coach/mentor	1, 9, 17	
Visionary/dreamer	2, 10, 18	
Commanding/directive	3, 11, 19	
Listener/collaborator	4, 12, 20	
People-focused/unifying	5, 13, 21	
Work-focused/production	6, 14, 22	

Use a hash mark (-) across vertical lines to indicate each leadership style assessment score. Connect the upper hash marks with a dotted line and do likewise to the bottom hash marks. The area between the ratings indicates leadership bandwidth; the areas outside the hash marks represent opportunities for improvement. (An example of a completed assessment diagram is shown in figure 3.4)

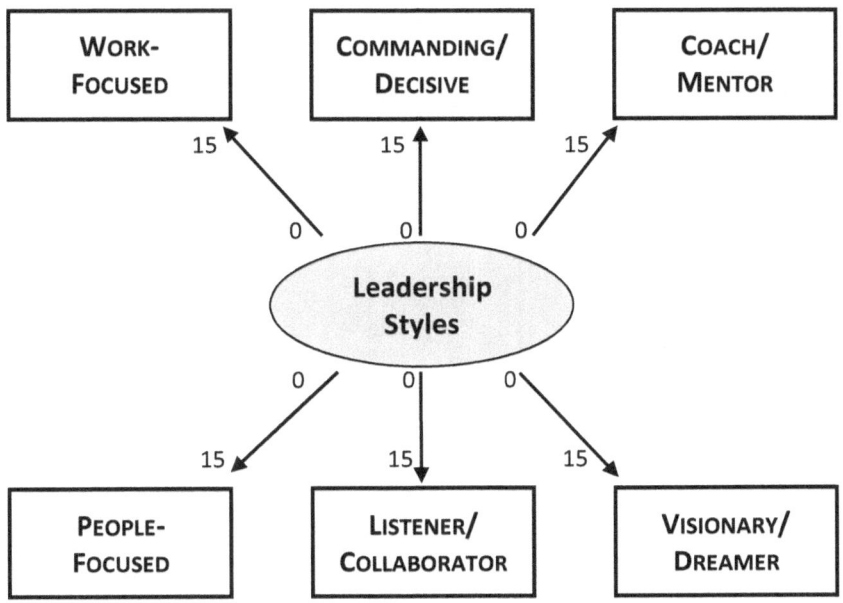

APPENDIX 2

PROCESS FOR DEVELOPING PERFORMANCE MEASURES

The process works like this: measures provide insight into performance; this insight enhances decision making; better decision making fosters performance, and improved performance creates public value and goodwill. Information from throughout the system is fed back into the performance measure process for maintenance and creation of new measures, and the process repeats itself.

As you will see, the process for developing performance measures is iterative. As a result, the steps to developing performance measures described below are not strictly sequential. An entity can begin a step, leave it, return to it later, verify completeness, and move on.

> ➢ Step 1: Use a collaborative process: The success of any performance measure effort depends on people working together to develop useful, specific, and realistic measures. Without commitment to a cooperative effort, performance measurement can become a paper exercise. But if done well, performance measurement can be a valuable monitoring, improvement, and evaluation tool.
>
> Performance measurement is a collaborative process designed to improve the quality, service, and efficiency of an entity. Therefore, it is wise to establish partnerships with those who will be providing the data, those who will be using the measures, and those who will

be influenced by the presence of the measures. Involve key sponsors, process/value stream owners, and customers (internal/external) in proposed measures, and discuss purpose and expectations of performance. Inclusion can help minimize or avoid unintended consequences. For performance measures to be taken seriously, key people must provide demonstrated commitment and support to the development and use of measures.

➢ Step 2: Decide on a framework. Improving performance requires a framework that helps entities perform, plan, improve, innovate, and react quickly to changing environments based on reliable, meaningful performance data. Whether an entity creates its own framework or chooses an existing one, successful implementation and use of measures require structure and method. Do not try to force fit a framework; do what makes sense and get started.

To get started, define your entity's primary/key deliverables. For each deliverable, define:
  o Key products, services, or activities
  o Primary inputs, key input requirements, and input suppliers/ sources
  o Primary outputs—products, services, or information, and key output characteristics
  o Key customers and/or customer groups, and their critical wants and needs
  o Desired outcomes
  o Critical support functions

Depending on the thoroughness of the entity's strategic plan, much of the above information may already be known. After all, wouldn't such information be good to know during the strategic planning effort? I think so.

The process of developing measures, collecting and recording measurements, and analyzing and interpreting performance data can be resource intensive. So before you collect the first piece of data, determine the data requirements of what you need to know by considering the following:

- o   Once you have defined key deliverables, collect related data. *What data do we need to describe and communicate performance?*
- o   By organizing and analyzing data, we gain information regarding the deliverables under study. *What does the data say?*
- o   Interpreting the data (in context and with user knowledge), we are able to gain knowledge regarding program performance. *What does the data mean?*

➢ Step 3: Developing measures: The first consideration in developing a performance measurement system should not be data collection. Instead identify the goals and objectives to be addressed by the measures. Without a guiding goal or objective, any reference for the measure is lost. Understanding what you want to measure is a prerequisite to developing meaningful measures of performance. When developing measures, consider the following:

- o   *Focus on important things.* Verify what is important, not just what is easy to measure or what has historically been measured.
- o   *Be selective.* It is easy to measure too much and the wrong things. All things being equal, fewer measures are better than more measures. Measure a balanced mix of performance— productivity, effectiveness, efficiency; accuracy, timeliness.
- o   *What gets measured gets done.* Make sure performance measures are linked to strategic planning elements (e.g., goals and objectives) and are useful for decision making. Consider both upstream and downstream performance measures to ensure the action taken for the good of one part of the entity does not come at the expense of or result in the downfall of another part.
- o   *Know your audience.* Measures should be based on the information needs of the receiver, and reflect his or her goals and objectives. Consider that different audiences may have different objectives for the same program. If so, different measures may be required. Knowing your audience goes a long way to ensuring that the intended receivers of your message are actually able to understand and use the information presented.

o *They have to understand it, in order to use it.* Constituents, employees, management, stakeholders, customers, etc., all have varying perspectives and interests.

o *Use sufficient measures.* It is rare that a single measure will provide a good description of a program and/or deliverable—multiple (two or more) measures are bound to provide descriptions that are more useful.

o *Quantitative, time-sequenced measures are best.* Design measures to show progress: *Is performance getting better, worse, or staying the same, and by how much?* If possible, avoid binomial measures (e.g., Yes/No, Complete/Incomplete). It is difficult to improve on *Yes* or *Complete.* If the evaluation is *No* or *Incomplete*, then by how much or to what degree should it be improved?

o *Understand the system.* Gain knowledge of the system and key deliverables, and consider the impact of the measures on people.

o *Align the measure with the message.* Different measures say different things. If the message is one of being good stewards of resources, then use an efficiency measure. If the message is of entity effectiveness, then use an outcome (effectiveness) measure.

➢ Step 4: Collect the data: implement a *data collection strategy*—a process to obtain performance data (measurements). The data collection strategy should be defined in conjunction with the measure. Special considerations include:

o **Operational definitions.** It is critical to define and standardize data collection.

o *Data quality.* Collect data so measures are comparable and understandable to the intended audience. Often, the most valuable performance data from a process is that which is obtained from personal observations. It is obvious, commonly cited, and frequently ignored: *data is only useful if the measurements are valid.* Data quality is crucial to credible analysis, meaningful information, and effective decision making.

o   *Beware of resistance and inattention.* Data collection can become biased or flawed if people do not support the measures or view them as a threat.

o   *Frequency of data collection.* Data collection frequency (e.g., daily, weekly, monthly) is dictated by the type of information sought, length of a process cycle, intended use, associated risks, consequences, and uncertainties. Data collection and reporting frequency need not be the same—collection may occur monthly but be reported quarterly.

o   *Costs of measures.* Consider the cost-benefits of data collection—the benefits of data collection should well outweigh the costs.

➤   Step 5: Use the data—analysis and charts: A key reason to measure performance is to meaningfully assess current performance and reasonably anticipate future performance. To that end, there is a big difference between data and useful information—there is ample evidence of collected data that is never used and of data used in statistics, tables, and charts that communicate nothing at all. Use what you collect; make what you say count.

Key to effective use and deployment of performance measures is to use them only where you have a purpose for them. Arbitrary use can have adverse effects. The presence of measures can actually change the way people do work.

o   *Know what you want, collect what you need, and use what you collect.* Frequently, important information contained in collected data is never revealed—the potential of data is untapped. As a result, powerful insights present in the data go unnoticed. Knowledge is squandered. Getting the most out of collected data involves a process for learning. Put learning to use on a small scale—test it, build competencies, then spread application and learning throughout the entity.

o   Though data management knowledge and skills vary by level and position, everyone needs a basic understanding of how to use, read, and interpret data. Use of data should not be a mystery or be relegated to the few.

- *Think ahead.* When developing measures and collecting measurements, have answers to: So what? Who cares? What am I going to do with it? How am I going to analyze it? Who is going to interpret it? If you never collected the data, who'd care? What effect would it have? How would product or service delivery be affected?
- *Feedback loops.* Performance results should be fed back into current and future strategic planning and budgetary processes and cycles. Collected data should demonstrate progress toward desired results or outcomes.
- *Baselines.* Data should be used to establish baselines for monitoring and assessing performance, and for evaluating improvements.
- *Use data to improve.* Sometimes measurements and analysis reveal less than desired performance. When it happens, verify the data and confirm the analysis, but do not shoot the messenger. Rather than searching for "who touched it last," find and fix the problem. Most often, the problem resides in the process, not the people.
- *Context.* The manner and extent to which entities achieve desired results must be interpreted in *context*—influencing factors (internal/external), policy/budget changes, etc.
- *Comparisons.* Compare entity performance to itself over time, to performance expectations, and to like entities.

➤ Step 6: Continually improve the measurement process: As mentioned, developing performance measures is an iterative process, not a one-time event. That means no matter how hard you work to develop and align a portfolio of meaningful measures, things are certain to change. As a result, the process for improving the performance of processes and systems also applies to performance measures—use it to ensure your measures make sense and measure the right things. Even so, realize that a delicate balance exists between measure consistency and continuous improvement.

Though one should be prepared to change measurement processes to respond to changing needs and priorities, it is very important to maintain some continuity in measures and data sets. Careful consideration should be given before changing any measure. Changes in measures may make some analyses difficult or impossible (e.g., comparisons, trends, forecasts).

APPENDIX 3

STRATEGIC PLANNING— ALIGNMENT AND DEPLOYMENT

Below is a simple example of strategic plan deployment—mission, goals, objectives, strategies, and tactics with accompanying measures of performance. I used a silly hypothetical—"Eliminate hostilities in the North Region"—so our focus would remain steadfast on process and flow; not sidetracked by real-world considerations. To accomplish their mission, strategic goals have been organized into five main regions: North, East, South, West, and Central. Below, we outline plan deployment for the North Region.

Strategic Planning—Level 1			
Goal: Eliminate hostilities in the North Region			
Objective		**Strategies**	**Performance Measure(s)**
1.0	Increase territory occupied by friendly forces to a minimum of 80% by end of year (Military High Command)	1.1 Decrease the # of castles occupied by the enemy (General A)	% of castles in enemy hands per month
		1.2 Decrease the time for deploying occupational forces (General B)	Elapsed time from notification to deployment per week
	What results are expected to be achieved?	1.3 Increase effectiveness of artillery ordinance (General C)	% of bombs that hit...
2.0	Decrease ...	2.1 ... How will results be achieved?	... How will you know if efforts are successful?
		2.2 ...	...

Notice that *Strategy 1.1* of Strategic Planning—Level 1 becomes the *Objective* of Strategic Planning—Level 2 (numbering remains the same).

Strategic Planning—Level 2				
	Objective		**Strategies**	**Performance Measure(s)**
1.1	Decrease the # of castles occupied by the enemy.	1.1.1	Significantly weaken the enemy fortifications (Colonel A)	# of castle walls still standing per day
	Performance Measure: % of castles in enemy hands per month	1.1.2	Reduce the enemy's firepower capability (Colonel B)	# of enemy artillery shells fired per hour per day
		1.1.3	Reduce the size of the enemy's ~~Level 2 is like Level 1 but on a smaller scale.~~	# of enemy troops within the castle per day
1.2	Decrease the time ...	1.2.1	...	...

Each *Strategy* of Strategic Planning—Level 3 then becomes the focus of Strategic Planning—Level 3.

Plan Deployment					
Strategy 1.1.1: Significantly weaken the enemy fortifications (Colonel A)					
	Tactics	**Timeframe**	**Responsible Person**	**Resources**	**Status**
1.1.1.1	Fire 105mm shells for 4 consecutive hours	DD/MM/YY 1600 hrs	Lt. A	26 rail-mounted artillery	Shells on order
1.1.1.2	Launch a barrage of proximity-fused shells at outer wall	DD/MM/YY 2000 hrs	Lt. B	25 long-range cannon	Testing new version of shells
1.1.1.3	Fire incendiary shells at major structures	DD/MM/YY 2200 hrs	Lt. C	500 incendiary shells	Squads conducting training maneuvers
Strategy 1...	Tactics	Timeframe	Responsible Person		
1.1.2.1	...	...	...	...	...

(cloud annotations: *What has to be done?* / *By when?* / *Who will do it?* / *What resources will be needed?* / *What is the stage of progress?*)

The mission is accomplished, in part, by aligning interdependent, mutually supporting, and reinforcing objectives, strategies, and performance measures. Note different parts of the organization support a common direction. When goals, objectives, strategies, and tactics are aligned, we are able to see the plan unfold—plan deployment.

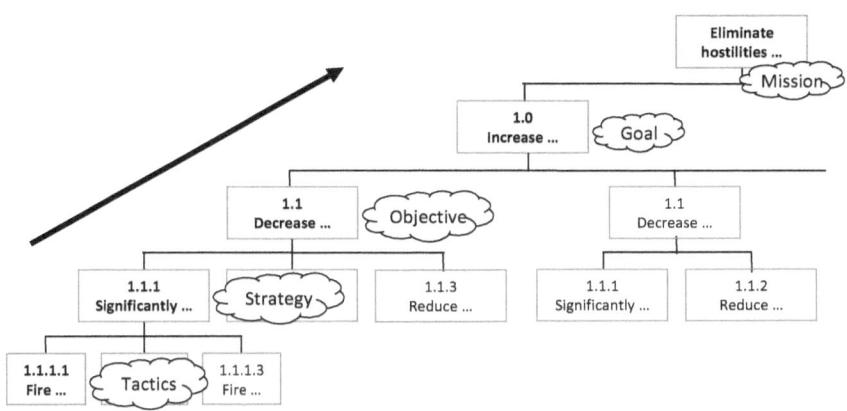

In plan deployment, we accomplish *tactics* to achieve a strategy, we accomplish *strategies* to achieve an objective, we accomplish *objectives* to achieve a goal, and accomplish *goals* to fulfill the *mission*. In the diagram above, we read from bottom-left to top-right.

In a field full of technical "how to" advice for managers, Marshall's emphasis of personal character on leadership is a refreshing and needed reminder for business professionals. **Jo VanDerSnick, Vice President, Commercial Banker, Middle Market Banking**

Leadership Nonnegotiables packs a lot in a small package. Whether you're new to leadership and looking to get started right, an already competent leader seeking to sharpen your skills, or an old hand who wants a go-to desk reference, this book is a great resource. It's rare to find anything that so thoughtfully and practically connects the dots between leadership and management. **Howard Schussler, serving as Government Services Director, the Lane County Council of Governments, Eugene, Oregon**

Nonnegotiable leadership is often missing in all levels of organizations/ leaders. Taking stock of one's leadership is of utmost importance for leadership success. This book establishes a course for leadership in the midst of change and reminds the reader/leader about staying the course and investing in the effort to bring mission and purpose back to the organization and to the mission statement. **Cheryl Ann Graf, ARNP, MSN, MBA; Carena Medical Group**

Personal character, leadership talent, and management skills are the three pillars that Dr. Marshall uses to summarize and articulate his wise and applied knowledge on leadership. Years of effective consulting grounds Dr. Marshall's approach on leadership, resulting in a very practical and useful book where everybody will find something to apply immediately. **Marc Correa, PhD, Executive Director of the Executive Masters, ESADE Business School**

www.ingramcontent.com/pod-product-compliance
Lightning Source LLC
Chambersburg PA
CBHW030854180526
45163CB00004B/1575